W9-BRH-156

There's a Beer in My Handbag

Unusual Thoughts about Everyday Faith

David O'Brien

CreateSpace
North Charleston, SC

"Dave eloquently recounts glimpses of God from his everyday life. Then, through the power of story, he invites us to savor our own God moments, grow in deeper intimacy with the Lord and serve God's people in greater fidelity." Jeanne Howard, Director, Office of Faith Formation, Catholic Diocese of Jackson

"David's experiences as well as those of his family serve to instruct the mind, challenge the heart and nurture the soul." Sr. Frances Sheridan, MSBT, Catholic Nursing Home chaplain.

"David O'Brien offers a very prophetic voice that provides everyday Christians unique insights into the depth of God's love for them and the challenge of a Christian life. His passion for justice and his personal desire to live his faith each day is imbedded in every chapter." Ann Marie Eckert, Center for Ministry Development

"My husband just finished reading aloud another chapter of your book. YOU HIT IT OUT OF THE PARK AGAIN! We keep copying chapters and sending them to friends and family." Melissa Rankin, Probation Officer

"My Mom told me she was at Mass this weekend with my brother. The Deacon was the homilist and Mom said that practically his whole homily was on a section from your book. Awesome again." Kristin Schwarz, Former Director of *Theology on Tap*, Cathedral, Chicago

"My husband and I were talking over Skype last night, because he is deployed now, and I read to him the chapter about the parking space. What a wonderful piece." Sandy Shepard

"I was amazed anyone could write so personal yet joyful a story about trusting and following the Divine Will. Wow. It reminded me of the book *He Leadeth Me* by Fr Walter J. Ciszek, S.J." Mary Rivers

THERE'S A BEER IN MY HANDBAG

Unusual Thoughts about Everyday Faith

There's a Beer in My Handbag
Unusual Thoughts about Everyday Faith

CreateSpace
7290 Investment Drive Suite B
North Charleston, SC 29418

ISBN-13: 978-1469987378
ISBN-10: 1469987376

The chapters of *There's a Beer in My Handbag* first appeared in the Archdiocese of Mobile's newspaper, *The Catholic Week* (www.mobilearchdiocese.org/catholicweek/). Many thanks to Archbishop Thomas J. Rodi and Larry Wahl, the newspaper editor, for allowing the Everyday Faith columns to be reproduced for this book. Also my sincerest gratitude to Gerald Darring and Rick Kopec for their support in making this book a reality.

To order copies of this book, go to:
www.createspace.com/3782468

David continues to write his bi-weekly column, which is available for syndication through *The Catholic Week* in Mobile, Alabama.

THERE'S A BEER IN MY HANDBAG

Unusual Thoughts about Everyday Faith

Contents

Entering Mission Territory

There is a church I visit sometimes that has a sign over the door that reads: "Entering Mission Territory." You can only read it when you are leaving the building. I appreciate the reminder that I am meant to be a missionary in my everyday life.

When you hear the word "missionary," do you think of Jesuits sent to convert indigenous tribes in the mountains of South America? Or Franciscans caring for the extreme poor in Africa or Asia?

You might even think of Protestants distributing bibles in Russia and China. But, in all honesty, do you wake up in the morning and think: "I am a missionary right here in my everyday life."

No? Me either.

When I wake up, I usually think: "Ugh, I'm still tired. Can I hit the snooze button again?"

Not very exotic.

Here's my problem though. That way of thinking makes mission work the task of a few world travelers who are usually priests, religious or maybe a college student doing a year of service. The rest of us have jobs, careers, studies, families, commitments and bills. Missionary work, according to that definition, doesn't easily fit into our reality.

You might think: "That's alright, I don't want to be a missionary. I prefer to volunteer at the parish when I have the time."

After the Second Vatican Council, thousands of lay people responded to the call to put our baptismal faith into action. We were enthused to have a place where we could serve. But since we grew up with priests and sisters exercising their ministries at Mass, in the Catholic

1

schools and with religious education, we assumed that those were the arenas where lay people should serve as well. Hence, in the decades following the Council, tens of thousands of us became lectors, catechists, choir members, school teachers, etc.

But is that really all there is for lay people? Are one or two hours a week the extent to which lay people are expected to live out their discipleship of Christ? What if I don't feel comfortable doing that type of ministry?

A priest recently explained it to me this way:

Ministry is the internal (or ecclesial) work of the Church which includes activities such as celebrating the sacraments, leading others in prayer and educating people in the faith. This is primarily the role of the hierarchy, the clergy, religious (sisters and brothers) and professional lay ministers.

Some lay people are called to serve in various roles at the parish level such as lectors, catechists and other ministries. But even for those lay people who do these ministries at the parish, ecclesial ministry is not their main job. Most of their time is spent at work or school, with family and friends.

Mission, on the other hand, is the work of the Church beyond the grounds of the parish. The *mission* of the Church is to bring Christ and His gospel to every place we are.

We go to church to receive the *ministry* that supports us in the work of the *mission*. Hearing the Word of God and receiving the Eucharist are meant to support the body of Christ—you and me--in the ongoing mission of Christ, which is to transform society into the Kingdom of God. In addition to Mass, we are strengthened for our work as missionaries in our everyday lives by attending bible studies, prayer groups, retreats and conferences.

At the end of Mass, the priest or deacon dismisses us saying some variation of: "the Mass is ended, go and announce the Gospel of the Lord" and we respond "thanks be to God." In effect, the Church that has gathered us is now sending us out into the mission fields.

We get the English word "Mass" from the Latin word *missio* which means "to be sent." Where are we being sent? To the people who need to know the love of Jesus. Will we be successful and always know what to do or say? Probably not. But next Sunday we will re-gather with other Catholic missionaries and share the stories of the mission. We will laugh at our screw ups, be encouraged by each other and celebrate our successes. We will receive the ministry of the ecclesial Church and be recharged by Word, Sacrament and community to be Christ's missionaries for another week.

Jesus invited his original disciples to be a part of his mission. He knew though that the mission would be impossible alone. Those early missionaries—and every generation since then--would need support and direction as well as structure and leadership, all guided by Christ's Spirit. So Jesus provided the basic building blocks for what would in time become the Church as we know it today.

In other words, the Church doesn't have a mission, the mission has the Church. We, the baptized, are both brought into the mission by the Church and sustained in our missionary calling by the Church. So while some will be ordained and others will take vows, all baptized Christians are part of the ongoing mission of Christ, every day and everywhere.

To paraphrase Msgr. Walter Niebrzydowski of New York City: All lay Christians are called to the mission and some are called to ministry. Lay ecclesial ministers help the clergy and religious proclaim and teach God's word; people in the mission show how to live it. Lay ministers help distribute the Body of Christ at Mass; lay people in the mission fields must become Christ's body in the world.

So if you find yourself in Target, McDonalds, the

supermarket or the movies, in your car or eating dinner with your family, remember you are Christ's missionary. Even if you never become a catechist or a lector, you are at the center of the Church's mission if you live your faith right where you are today.

In the pages that follow are essays about my attempts as a lay person to live as a missionary in my everyday life. Some of the chapters are about the church. Many more are about my life in the world as a husband, a father, a worker, a neighbor, an American, a friend, a brother and a Catholic Christian in the 21st century.

I hope as you read you will stop to consider your own life, with all the challenges and blessings you experience each time you enter mission territory.

There's a Beer in My Handbag

I teach a Theology for Ministry course at Spring Hill College. In addition to a weekly one-hour seminar with me, the students participate in various ministry internships somewhere in the community.

During a recent class discussion, one student recounted how over the summer he and his mother were approached by an elderly homeless woman as they exited the local Winn Dixie supermarket.

"Excuse me," she said as she waddled up next to their grocery cart, carrying all her worldly belongings. "Would you happen to have a few dollars to spare? I'm really hungry but I don't have any money."

The student and his mother rifled through their pockets and pulled out a few bucks, maybe five or six singles. They handed them to the old lady and tried to communicate the Christian compassion in their hearts.

"I hope this will tide you over," prayed his mother.

"Here," added the student, "take our bananas too," as he pulled out their newly purchased *Chiquitas* from their cart and handed them over.

She thanked them graciously and left them with a benediction: "God bless you for your kindness to an old woman. May Jesus repay you back one hundredfold."

Duly blessed, they made their way across the expansive parking lot until they reached their car and unloaded their overflowing cart into the trunk.

"Mom," the student blurted out. "I don't think that woman has any way to carry those bananas. Let me run this bag over to her. I just saw her come out of the store."

When he reached her sitting on the bench in front of the store, the handbag on her lap lay open and he noticed some newly purchased beers poking out. She scrambled to throw her jacket over the bag, obviously embarrassed by the incriminating evidence.

"I thought you might need something to carry your bananas," he offered, choosing not to mention the beers in her handbag.

She thanked him awkwardly, trying to cut short the conversation.

He didn't know if she realized he had seen her liquid lunch. Quickly he turned and made his way back to his mother.

This episode raised many questions for the class. Should we give money to street people who ask or are we simply feeding their addictions? Will God judge us on what they do with our money or on what we do with our money? By supporting this type of panhandling, are we simply enabling their dead end lifestyle instead of pointing these lost souls to the social service agencies where they could get some real help?

All these questions were legitimate and fruitful for theological reflection. But I couldn't get past that painful picture of the old woman sitting on the bench with those beers in her handbag, caught, red-handed in her dishonesty and addiction.

I thought about how unworthy she was of my student's generosity and how she had betrayed his charity and goodwill.

In that very moment, like a flash, my mind flipped the scene. Instead of the old woman on the bench, there I was asking God for one of a hundred different things. I expected God to help me. I anticipated He would. I knew He knew my need. He had always helped me in the past. But as the Lord walked over, I looked down and noticed I had beers in my handbag.

There they were as clear as day. I knew the Lord saw them too. In fact, in that moment, I knew that the Lord always saw them, every time I asked and expected Him to respond to my need.

My sins, my faults, my petty excuses for why I didn't always do what I promised to do, there they were. I looked up at the Lord and felt ashamed. I remembered how many times I had said one thing to God and then did another, each time giving into my addictions, my fears, my desire for comfort or momentary pleasure.

Gently, the Lord reached over and touched my slumping shoulder. I didn't look up at Him, hoping not to prolong the moment. And then, with great tenderness, He answered my prayer. It occurred to me that He always saw the beers in my handbag and He always chose to love me anyway, each time looking past my history of unworthiness and instead inviting me into His world of generosity.

I looked up at Him and realized that His eyes carried no judgment. Only love. My guilt retreated and I felt only gratefulness. Why He loved me like that, I do not know. But I was grateful He did.

As my mind returned to the classroom, I mentioned to the class that no matter what we did in ministry, whether at a parish, a hospital or with the homeless, we should try to remember that we are no better than the people with whom we minister. We all have beers in our handbag and we always will. Still, somehow, with incomprehensible generosity and graciousness, God continues to bless us, even though we do not deserve it. All we are doing is passing along His love. Nothing more.

You May Board Now, Mr. O'Brien

So much of being Catholic has little to do with formal prayer or Mass or anything overtly religious. A good portion of living our faith is about how we respond when things go wrong.

Take for example this past week when I attended a conference for work. All went well until thunderstorms and tornadoes delayed my early morning flight—think 5 a.m. wake up—out of St. Louis.

I sat in the airport and watched the departure screen change from 7 a.m. to 12:30 p.m. in fifteen minute increments. Each change elicited a moan from the crowd. After another round of cell phone calls, the latest cadre of antagonized people lined up to assault the helpless gate agents.

I struck up a few conversations with my disgruntled airport neighbors, trying to focus on the positives—"I just had a green tea frappacino from the *Starbucks* at Gate 13 and it was delicious. Do you drink tea?" When my conversation partners stood up and left, I didn't take it personally. "Probably going to *Starbucks* for a green tea," I'd tell myself.

The plane finally left St. Louis but when I arrived in Chicago the plasma TV board alerted me that it was time for another frappacino. CANCELLED is the word that filled the board, sending thousands of travelers scrambling for new flights, hotels and answers.

"Remain calm, breathe and talk to the Lord," I repeated like a mantra. "Call your wife, call work and find some help." I had to consciously choose not to contribute to the dark cloud of anger and frustration enveloping the airport. This is especially difficult when the airlines blame God for the cancellations and offer little assistance.

Through it all, even though nobody in the airport knew I worked for the church, I felt I didn't betray my commitment to Christ. I remained patient and friendly, showing courtesy to the many stressed out people all around me.

Then it happened. My new flight from Chicago arrived in Atlanta 15 minutes before my connection to Pensacola. I sprinted through the airport, bags in tow, to my gate. Feeling a surge of triumph as I approached the agent, I almost expected her to congratulate me for making it this far. Instead, she told me that Chicago neglected to check me all the way through. Consequently, they gave away my seat assignment because I wasn't at the gate 15 minutes before the flight.

"Remain calm, breathe and talk to the Lord." It was all I could do as thoughts raced inside my head: "Violence won't help here nor will tears. Even if this woman knows nothing about my life, my job or my faith, God knows. Am I going to allow myself to get swept away in this moment of injustice, stupidity, hunger and sleep deprivation? Was it this unsympathetic woman's fault that I am stranded again? Probably yes, but I shouldn't strangle her. What if she has small children? Maybe I need to go somewhere and pray before I lose it."

In a surge of grace, I walked away to regather myself. After a moment, I returned to the gate agent and calmly asked if I could do anything to avoid the reoccurrence of this situation in the future?

Just then, like an angel of light sent directly from heaven to Gate 37, the other agent who heretofore had remained silent, spoke up: "You may board now, Mr. O'Brien."

I could have hugged her. I wanted to share with her my saga and how she was the first kind soul to cross my path in days. But I simply thanked her as I boarded and thanked God for the grace of that simple assistance.

Faith permeates our everyday situations. When

things go our way, there is praise and thanks to God. When things fall apart, there is patience and trust in the Lord. But through it all, there is the consistent witness of Jesus, who loved those who helped him and even those who hurt him. He respected and honored those who deserved disdain. How many people noticed this about him during his life, were impressed and chose to follow him? How many of us still notice today? It is a great gift to be invited to live like Christ. I am convinced it is the only way the world can be saved.

Tips for Everyday Faith

When things don't go your way or you are faced with a crisis, ask these simple questions: *where is God in this situation?* and *What is God trying to teach me in this?* Then gently listen for a word or insight from God.

Are You Catholic Enough?

That is a hard question to answer. Who decides? What are the criteria? What are the benefits if you pass the test? What happens if you don't?

The question may not appear relevant except it seems to be coming up more and more these days. Take, for example, the pamphlet circulating in parishes entitled: *Voting Guide for Serious Catholics.* I read the pamphlet and was happy that I qualified for "serious" status according to the author.

Or how about the websites that rate your orthodoxy based on where you work, with whom you associate and to whom you minister. I wonder how long it will be until I show up on such a website because something I said was deemed unacceptable by their webmaster. Somehow I cannot see Jesus setting up such a website; probably because he hung around the unorthodox too much.

Now I understand this emphasis on conformity with official church doctrine. Nothing is more disingenuous than a Catholic politician courting the Catholic vote while publicly disavowing fundamental Church teaching. That kind of hair splitting—"personally opposed but..."—should result in an immediate disqualification from public office.

Moreover, for too many years our U.S. Catholic culture, and in particular our Catholic universities, resisted the hierarchy and discredited many of the teachings coming out of Rome.

Thank God those days are moving into the rearview mirror. Younger Catholics are not invested in the issues that proved so divisive and distracting to previous generations. Catholic universities now offer their considerable resources to further the mission of the local church.

Still, the orthodoxy police make me nervous.

I spoke with a Catholic woman in her 20's the other day. She attends my parish and appreciates the excellent music and the challenging preaching. But she admits that she is trying to find her place in the Catholic community.

"I have gone to other parishes for Mass and tried to join groups for people my age," she describes, "but I always get the feeling that I am not Catholic enough."

Unlike some Protestant churches that are communities for the saved, Catholicism holds on to Jesus' vision that insisted that there are many mansions in the Father's house. (John 14:2) In other words, the Catholic genius is that we make room for people who are struggling with their faith, people who are not quite there yet.

Maybe that fills our churches with parishioners who are too lukewarm for some. But haven't we all had moments when we needed the community to carry us along, when we had our doubts, lost our focus or mixed up our priorities?

In the end, the journey of faith is both personal and communal, one part passionate sprint, one part long distance discipline. Evangelization and catechesis work in tandem to help us grow ever closer to Christ, who embraces saints and sinners, and recommends we let the wheat and the weeds grow together. (Mt 13:30) By that criteria, we all just might be Catholic enough.

Tips for Everyday Faith

Are there people in your life who are estranged from the Church or reluctant to return to their Catholic roots? Spend some time really listening to them and where they are at in their faith journey. Chances are they are searching for something to fill the void but don't feel welcome in the Catholic community. Studies have shown that most people who stay away from church mention feeling judged as a main reason. Perhaps you can be the person who makes room for their questions and complaints with the loving kindness of the Lord.

Tastes Like Jesus

When my wife, Rachel, and I were expecting our first child, I took up the practice of blowing on Rachel's womb after I received communion at Mass. I don't know from where the idea came. I just wanted our baby to be blessed by the Lord even though she wasn't even born yet.

Since Clare's birth day, I've continued this little tradition with her and now I include her two little brothers, Toby and Joshua, in the Eucharistic blessing. They all love it and look forward to Daddy "blowing Jesus" on them. Rachel thinks I'm weird.

Toby, about a year ago, started opening up his mouth when I did this, like a baby bird awaiting the worm his mother had brought back to the nest. Last Sunday, when I blew the Eucharist on him, he said: "Tastes like Jesus."

On another occasion, when I came home from an event where I drank a glass of wine, Clare said, "Daddy, you smell like Jesus."

Their childlike words started me thinking. Could I identify all the places I encountered Jesus? That kindly person who went out of his way to affirm me for a job well done "sounds like Jesus." The lady who hugged that crying woman in the back of the church, I bet she "felt like Jesus". That teacher who lovingly works with the holy terror in her class even though he drives her crazy; she surely is "patient like Jesus." I came up with a thousand examples: he emails like Jesus, she drives like Jesus, they love each other after 47 years of marriage like Jesus, and he runs his business like Jesus.

Then, the other day when I was away from home giving a talk at a parish, my wife called to tell me about her day. She said someone knocked on the front door around 4 p.m. The kids pulled back the curtains and started saying, "Mommy, it's our friend, it's our friend." Rachel opened the door to find a local homeless man standing in the doorway. Our family knows Joseph because he "lives" out and about in the area and we see him. I usually say hello and exchange a few pleasantries. He seems harmless and he is friendly towards the children. Standing face to face with Joseph, Rachel's first reaction was to shut the door and call the police. What was he doing, knocking on our door? My wife, who is not a big person and tends to be naturally fearful, felt especially threatened because I was a few hours away giving my talk.

But the children were so excited. "Our friend is here," they said. How could Rachel close the door on him now, with them standing by her side, watching?

"Hello Joseph, how are you?" she said. "I'm fine," he replied, adding, "but I was wondering if you could give me a little food. I'm waiting on my Social Security check and I'm so hungry."

Rachel suggested a grilled cheese and when he nodded his head yes, she asked him to wait on the porch while she put it together. Back in the kitchen, she thought about this poor, old man. It was so hot outside, over 100 degrees. Where did he go to get a break from the heat? She grabbed a 64 oz cup from the cupboard and filled it with ice and cold water. Handing him the sandwich and the drink, she wished Joseph's well and included, "stay cool," even though she knew that was hopeless in this heat.

I listened to my wife and thought about how normally her fears about personal safety can paralyze her. I thought about how difficult it must have been for her to get past her need for self-protection. And, I marveled at how she shifted gears so quickly, forgetting her own discomfort with the presence of this homeless man at her front door and instead focused on Joseph's life and how uncomfortable he must be. Finally, I thought about my children and the great gift they gave both my wife and me with their openness to this hurting man at our door.

So I've added a few more phrases to my list: knocks on my door like Jesus; makes friends like Jesus; faces her fears like Jesus; and gives drinks to the thirsty like Jesus (Matthew 25:35).

Joseph showed up on our front door again a few days later. This time I was home and answered the door.

"Hello Joseph," I greeted him. "How are you doing?"

"Doing alright, doing alright," he responded, eyes focused on the ground. "I wanted to return the cup your wife gave me the other day."

"Thank you," I replied. "I'll fill it up for you again. You can keep it."

"Would you have another grilled cheese sandwich too?" he inquired. I told him I'd see what I could find.

After I sent Joseph off with another cup of ice water and a sandwich, I realized I needed to talk with my wife about how we were going to respond to Joseph if he kept coming to our house for food. My heart broke for this man, to be without a home at his age, out in this heat walking the streets. I thought about how Mother Teresa said that we should see Jesus in the "distressing disguise of the poor." Was Jesus coming to my door asking for a grilled cheese sandwich? But then I considered the safety of my wife and children. Joseph seems harmless but I don't really know him. Something is not right or he wouldn't be living on the streets. Is it drugs? Does he suffer with mental illness? Perhaps he has episodes that make him violent or dangerous? Was it fair to my wife to put her at risk by allowing Joseph to keep coming to our home?

So many questions filled my mind. I kept vacillating between guilt, helping Joseph out of Christian charity, and wanting to make sure my family was reasonably safe. Moreover, I know my neighbors are sensitive to the presence of the homeless in the area. They support the local shelters and they don't see any reason why people need to be knocking on our doors looking for handouts. I could see their point too.

Later that evening when Rachel and I talked, we agreed that if Joseph returned I would recommend that he go to the local social service agencies for his meals. I rehearsed what I would say, trying to be as kind as possible and respectful of Joseph's dignity. I certainly did not want him to feel as if we didn't care about him. It's just that we were not comfortable with him coming to our door like this.

Three weeks have passed and still no signs of Joseph. Will he come back? I don't know. Did we make the right decision? I wonder. Perhaps it was enough that we treated Joseph like a human being when he came to our door those two times. But maybe God is just giving us more time to reconsider our decision before He shows back up at our door again.

The Face of Mental Illness

We have a national celebrity in our Archdiocese. She has received national awards, been written up in national magazines and spoken to audiences large and small across the country. Most impressively, she shares her giftedness for free, living in gospel simplicity, devoting herself totally to God and her mission.

What exactly is her claim to fame? What are her unique gifts that bring her such acclaim? Surprisingly, it is her mental illness. Lucindia Claghorn suffers with paranoid schizophrenia.

As a third order secular Franciscan, a devoted student of theology and a full-time volunteer for various social service agencies, Lucindia sees her sickness as the source of her ministry.

"I have paid a heavy personal and professional price for being open about my mental illness," explains Lucindia. "But the Lord has called me to advocate for better treatment of the mentally ill and a greater acceptance of those who live with mental disorders."

According to those in mental health ministry, misconceptions, stereotypes and discrimination against the mentally ill are still very prevalent in society and in the Church today.

One person with mental health issues said, "The stigma is harder to deal with than the illness itself." For example, people are able to write "diabetic" on job applications without fear of a negative reaction. But to admit to any level of mental illness would immediately eliminate the hope of landing most jobs.

Lucindia challenges the Church and society to see those with mental illness as Pope John Paul II described them: "bearers of God's image and likeness. (People with) the inalienable right not only to be considered ... an image of God and therefore ... a person, but also to be treated as such."

"People are afraid of mental illness because it effects what makes us most human, our brain and our personalities," contends Lucindia. "People feel threatened because they don't understand that mental illness is just that, an illness."

Few realize that mental health infirmities are the most common of all sicknesses, far more common than cancer, diabetes, heart disease or arthritis. The National Institute of Mental Health estimated that one out of four families in the U.S. has a loved one with a serious mental illness. Despite the prevalence of such disorders, people don't want to fund research and treatment for mental illness, according to Lucindia. "What hurts is that our jails and prisons have become the de facto mental hospitals. Can you imagine if they did that to people with cancer?"

This reluctance to deal with mental illness may stem from the mistaken belief that the mentally ill are violent and dangerous. Low budget slasher movies that depict the mentally ill as murderous psychotics have fueled this misperception for decades. Antipathy towards the mentally ill might even go back to the days when society and the church believed the mentally disabled were possessed by the devil or being punished by God.

National statistics, however, indicate that those with mental illness are far more likely to be victims of violent crime than the perpetrators of vicious attacks.

According to the World Health Organization there are 450 million people in the world affected by neurological or behavioral mental disorders, of which 873,000 commit suicide each year.

Pope Benedict XVI called mental illness "a true health and social emergency."

Deacon Tom Lambert, a spokesperson for Chicago's

mentally ill, invites the Church to see the gifts of all the members of the Body of Christ. "At a recent Archdiocesan meeting on disabilities (in Chicago) there were people in wheelchairs, people who were blind, people who were deaf and people who were mentally ill," he described. "They were there because they were leaders, not because they were people with diseases or disabilities. One is a motivational speaker, another runs parish programs, another heads a program to distribute medical supplies. All were people letting the works of God be visible through them. The purpose of the meeting was to spread the word about the ABILITIES of all God's people. To tell us that people should be known not by their diseases or illnesses or disabilities but by the gifts they have to offer."

Lucindia would agree. "I want to be the face of mental illness to the public so people will see that with proper medication and treatment, the mentally ill can function, do well and make a meaningful contribution to society."

Tips for Everyday Faith

When you pray the *Sorrowful Mysteries of the Rosary*, use the mystery of "Jesus is crowned with thorns" to pray for those who suffer with any sickness of the mind.

www.everybodyswelcome.org.uk/mentalhealth

This website from England offers some helpful resources for those interested in the pastoral care of the mentally ill within the Catholic community.

Searching for the Right Person

There are two burning questions that dominate the lives of young adults: what am I supposed to do with my life and with whom should I do it? Purpose and community.

For most, the second question is about finding the right person. Will I ever get married? How will I find my soulmate? Is there just one 'right person' or are there many options? Has God handpicked one person for me or is the choice up to me? If God is sending someone my way, how do I recognize him/her?

I spent many tortured nights wrestling with these questions. My journey included seven years discerning between the priesthood and marriage, a year in a Franciscan seminary, almost nine years in a relationship that led to a marriage proposal then ended in a painful broken engagement.

Honestly, at that point, I began to lose hope. Was God even listening anymore? Worn out by years of trying, I decided to give up and just be content, if not happy, with being single.

A year later at a young adult prayer group, I saw an unknown face in the crowd. She introduced herself as Rachel from Pensacola, new to New Jersey for a year of missionary work. She mentioned that she was also thinking about becoming a Trinitarian sister.

Intrigued by her beauty, her warm personality and her obvious commitment to her faith, I thought about saying hi during the social hour after the program. But with my heart still too beat up from the end of my engagement, I decided against it. Why bother? She was obviously not in the market for a relationship.

The next day I mentioned Rachel to Kate, a very

spiritual friend of mine. Kate seemed to have a special frequency between her and Jesus. She often stopped looking at me when we talked and stared off into the distance, as if she were a dog listening to a high pitched whistle. When I told her about Rachel and how I wasn't going to bother, she did that Jesus dog whistle thing again.

I asked her, "Kate, what? Why are you doing that?"

She responded cryptically: "I would pay attention to this girl, David."

I dismissed the idea but deep inside, I wondered.

Some weeks later at a young adult picnic, I invited Rachel to join my team for the volleyball tournament. Being less than 5 feet tall, I thought she could benefit from my athletic prowess. She declined saying she already joined a team. A little disappointed, I figured she would regret her decision when my team slaughtered her team on the court.

I soon found out though that Rachel was an Olympic quality player and her team was decimating all the competition in large measure because of her.

When we finally faced each other in the championship round, she abused us without mercy. Desperate for a way to knock her off her game, I tried to get inside her head by saying: "You are great. Too bad that once you miss a shot, it's all down hill from there."

A few points later, Rachel amazingly missed a point, and then another, then another. We mounted a furious comeback and took the lead. Feeling cocky, I whispered across the net to Rachel: "Mental toughness."

The ball was served, back and forth, over the net several times until it rested just above the net between Rachel and me. I catapulted myself as high as I could, only to receive a volleyball sandwich. Rachel out jumped me and spiked the ball right in my face. Her team never lost another point. Game, set, match. I was starting to like this girl.

Later that night back at the missionary house, Rachel shockingly revealed to me that she had been praying and journaling about us. "Us", I thought. There was no "us". But as I listened to her, I felt an emerging love in my heart that I had been suppressing out of fear.

We ended up in the chapel for the next two nights talking until 4 a.m. We talked about our dreams, our families, our faith and our past disappointments. It wasn't long before we recognized that something was happening, something bigger than either one of us. God's hidden hand was beginning to show itself.

It was as if we were sitting in a theater watching the curtain open on a new Broadway play. The orchestra played the overture. We knew that behind the curtain the scene had been set. But oh, the wonder and awe of seeing that curtain peel back to reveal what lay behind it.

All these years, God had been arranging the scenes of our lives and now the curtain was finally opening for us to see. It was all there, miraculously.

Neither one of us had been previously married. Both had seriously considered religious life. What she wanted I wanted and my dreams matched hers.

At one point on the second night, out of curiosity, I asked her what kind of wedding she wanted. She responded: "I'd like everyone to be there and maybe there would be a potluck reception." Her words brought me back to the person I had once hoped to be.

For years I had talked about a potluck reception as a way to live the gospel, espousing simplicity and avoiding the excesses of the wedding industry in New Jersey. My ideas though were met by the mockery and derision of friend and family alike. Even my mother once told me that no woman would ever want to marry me if I talked like that.

During my previous relationship, my potluck reception idea was such a source of conflict, I eventually abandoned it, succumbing to the pressure of the over the top, limited guest list, $60,000+ Princess Di wedding reception.

But here was Rachel, unbeknownst to her, speaking the very words I had once said. I sensed the Lord's tender love piercing my heart. He said to me: "I know you thought I had forgotten you but I never did. Don't you know how much I love you? I heard every word you ever prayed."

In that moment, I realized that Rachel was an expression of God's love for me and that to marry her would be the way God was inviting me to grow in His love. I burst into tears. She was the one. She was God's gift to me.

Back in the chapel the next night I asked Rachel, again out of curiosity, not as a proposal, "are you going to marry me?" Without hesitation she glibly replied: "I think I am." To which I said, "I think you are."

We will be nine years married this August, with our fourth baby due that same month. But we are no more certain today than we were in the chapel that night. God made it abundantly clear that He had been with us every step of the way. He still is.

I cannot say that the manner in which this played out in my life is the way God will act for others. But I do know this. Single, married, lonely, searching, divorced, hurting or feeling abandoned. You are not alone. God is not only watching you. God is actively working to bring you the love and the happiness you have always dreamed about.

What that will look like, I do not know. But if you can trust Him, God will get you there. Guaranteed. (John 10:10) The truth is, God's dream for you is probably better than anything you could have ever asked for or imagined.

Ten Things I Love About Rome

Have you ever taken a pilgrimage to Rome? If you haven't, it is the type of trip that can change your spiritual life and solidify your Catholic identity.

I visited Rome once as a college student during a semester abroad and then again years later for a friend's ordination. Both visits hold cherished memories for me: Christmas Eve Midnight Mass at St. Peter's Basilica with Pope John Paul II; a sumptuous lunch at the Cecilia Metella Restaurant which lasted so long it became dinner; and a tour given by my friend of the excavations underneath St. Peter's Basilica, a tour which ends at the bones of St. Peter.

As they say: "You don't discover Rome, you remember it."

Rome is a city that belongs to everyone. It is not just a modern metropolis but a spectacular history book written in stone; a huge, inhabited work of art.

Here are 10 things I love about the city that once headquartered an empire that stretched from Scotland to the Sahara.

1) More powerful and enduring than the Roman Empire is the faith that sprung from Rome. The seeds of Christianity were watered here by the blood of the early martyrs including Sts. Peter and Paul.

2) In Rome you can visit and pray at the two great Basilicas built where Peter and Paul were killed: St. Paul Outside the Walls and St. Peter's on Vatican Hill.

3) Rome is the city that Michelangelo sculpted, Raphael painted and where Bernini made bronze come to life.

4) The Basilica of St. Mary Major owes its existence to a

miracle. It is said that in the 4th Century the Virgin Mary asked to have a church built in an area which she would cover with snow. The next day it snowed even though it was summer in Rome. On August 5 every year, white rose petals are scattered from the Basilica dome in memory of the miracle.

5) Two other reasons to visit St. Mary Major Basilica: it holds the relics of the manger of the child Jesus and its ceiling is made with the first gold from the New World brought over from Christopher Columbus.

6) The Vatican was declared an independent state in 1929 although it is only 100 acres wide and still includes only 700 passport holders.

7) St. Peter's Basilica is the largest church in the world with room for 60,000 worshippers. It includes 450 statues and 50 altars. It took 120 years to complete during which 20 different Popes held the Chair of Peter.

8) St. Peter's Square holds 284 columns and 140 saints. As a symbol of the Catholic Church, the colonnade opens up like two arms embracing the world.

9) The Egyptian obelisk in the square is said to be the last thing a dying St. Peter saw in Nero's Circus Maximus as he hung upside down crucified on a cross.

10) In a city where all roads lead to eternity, Rome is a place to marvel at the past and recommit to the journey toward the eternal City of God.

I hope to return to Rome someday with my wife and children. Nothing I could ever tell them at home could compare with the experience of seeing our rich Catholic history and tradition come to life like it does on the streets of Rome.

Raising Faithful Kids: I Need Help

Amazingly, the summer came and went before we had a chance to catch our breath. The schools are back in session and the routines of the academic year are falling into place. Even my little girl is enrolled in an art class at the museum already. Wasn't she wearing diapers last week?

Our new Archbishop recently wrote about the relationship between parents, Catholic schools and parish religious education programs in regards to the Catholic education and formation of our children. He stated:

"It is important to remember that our Catholic schools and parish religious education programs are not meant to replace the efforts of parents, but to assist parents in the Catholic education which must first and always be present within the family."

The emphasis on the critical role of the parents in passing on the faith is clear. Schools and parish programs were never designed to take over the role of parents in the faith formation of our children. They supplement and support the consistent and conscious efforts of parents to make our Catholic faith substantial and integral in the upbringing of our children.

Parenthood is a high calling, a great responsibility given to us by God. My children, God help them, are dependent upon me to not only model Christ to them but to bring them into the rich life of our Catholic faith. That seems overwhelming when so often I can't even get them to eat their dinner or stop hitting each other. I need help. We all do.

Into this gap, this void where parents fall short of providing what every child deserves, steps our Catholic community. The Church, as an institution, values our children and their religious education so highly that we dedicate billions of dollars around the world to support families in raising Catholic kids.

The history of the Church shines with its commitment to education and formation. Beginning with the early Christian monasteries, the story of our organized investment in Catholic faith formation is impressive. Consider all the sisters and brothers who made Catholic schools, universities and "CCD" a staple of the church's life. Or the legions of dedicated lay people who now selflessly serve as parish catechists and Catholic school teachers.

Even Mother Teresa began her work with the poor of Calcutta by teaching children to write in the dirt with a stick.

Catechesis is a preeminent commitment we have as a Catholic community. A short list of all the ways the church teaches the faith to the young includes: homilies, Children's Liturgy of the Word, Vacation Bible Schools, universities, high schools, parish schools, religious education programs, youth ministries, high school and college campus ministries, and sacramental formation.

Canon Law itself states that every pastor is obliged to provide catechesis. *(Canon 776)*

So I embrace my moral obligation to form my children, by word and example, in the faith and practice of the Christian life. But I am so grateful for our Church and the support systems that are in place. Together I hope we can lead our children to know and love God now and be with God forever in heaven.

Over a Parking Spot

Humility is a desirable virtue. It confronts our egos, reminds us not to take ourselves too seriously and curtails our tendency to overvalue our opinions. Nothing is more obnoxious than a person who thinks their way is the only way, their truth is the Truth. That kind of arrogance is hard to be around.

A person who exudes humility, on the other hand, is everyone's friend. He recognizes and affirms the giftedness of others. He is quick to forgive when offended because he knows he has hurt many along the way through his stupidity and sin.

Humbleness avoids the temptation to over assert one's rights — "How dare she talk to me like that!" "Don't they know who I am?" or "He can't treat me like that."

Humility accepts inconvenience for the good of others.

I want God to teach me to be humble, meek and poor in spirit (Mt 5:3, 5). But, ugh, I hate it when He answers that prayer.

Last week, my family attended a children's event at a museum. I arrived ahead of my wife and kids and I found an open parking spot for them. Rachel asked me to save it for her as she would arrive in less than one minute. As I hung up the cell, a Honda Civic going the wrong way down a one way street raced up to the parking spot. I stood in the space and watched the driver begin to back towards me. Holding my hands up, I directed the person to stop. The guy behind the wheel abruptly jumped out of the car and aggressively confronted me. His wife, children and mother-in-law watched from the car as he struck his best Alpha male pose.

Shocked and somewhat unnerved, I explained that I

was saving the spot for my wife. I pointed to our minivan and said: "She is right there."

"My car is right here," he countered.

"But I'm standing in this spot," I noted, trying to remain calm.

"Fine," he rebutted as he turned back to his car. "Keep standing there while I run you over."

Not quite sure I had heard the guy right, I watched as he re-engaged his car and backed up directly towards me.

I quickly stepped aside and thought, "What a jerk!"

As I walked around the corner to my wife's new parking spot, I told myself, "I should've videotaped him with my phone and then sued him for hitting me."

My wife was equally offended when I told her what happened. "Here, you carry the baby so he will feel bad when he sees that we have a newborn."

"Yeah," I thought. "Too bad my wife isn't nine months pregnant."

We bumped into a handicapped friend on the way into the museum. Now, I couldn't wait to see that guy again inside. An infant and a person in a wheelchair. When he sees us, he might just burst into tears and confess to me how much of a loser he is.

These thoughts dominated my mind for nearly an hour until I realized I was obsessing and prayed to let go of my anger and desire for revenge. I thought I had put it behind me but when I returned to my car I had to fight the urge to slash the guy's tires before I left.

Now, I don't know what you call these thoughts and desires, but they don't fall under the category of humility. Instead of enjoying my children, I spent my energy hating, being offended and acting as if my whole world was collapsing. Over what? A parking spot.

Admittedly, this guy's behavior was inappropriate. But what exactly was Christ-like about my response? How did my attitude mirror that of Jesus who had railroad spikes hammered into him and then forgave the guys who did it?

I am not proud of myself for how I reacted. Still, I am grateful to God because He has shown me how far I still need to go. Even my four-year-old son seems more humble than me. When he later encountered the guy in the museum, he said: "Isn't that the man who was mean to Daddy?" My wife answered yes, adding: "And what do we do to people who treat us badly?" Without thinking twice my son offered, "We treat them with kindness." Now that takes humility.

Tips for Everyday Faith

I pray a "Litany of Humility" regularly that includes lines like: "Deliver me Jesus from the desire of being honored. Deliver me Jesus from the fear of being wronged. Jesus, grant me the grace to desire that others may increase and I may decrease." It is a hard prayer but a great prayer. Google it.

I Hate to Lose

On these high Holy Days of our Catholic tradition, I have to make a confession. I hate to lose. I am competitive by nature. My wife knows not to talk to me if my team loses. She doesn't understand my prehistoric, monosyllabic grunts anyway so she just leaves me alone. I just like to win.

Even when I am wrong, I have a hard time admitting it. Instead, I find the weakness in the other person's argument and formulate my counterattack.

That is why Good Friday bothers me. I'd be happy to skip right to Easter Sunday and the winner's circle. Jesus may have been knocked down on Friday but he came back with a vengeance by Sunday. He's a winner on Sunday and we all like winners.

But is that what Easter is all about: winning? Was the great victory really accomplished on Sunday morning or was the real triumph on Friday afternoon on that cross?

Oh that cross ... it just bothers me.

I don't know if I like the fact that he was innocent and he didn't defend himself in court. Why didn't he let his disciples pull their swords and fight for him in the garden? He knew what lay ahead of him–torture, ridicule, abandonment and a shameful public execution. Why didn't he call on the armies of heaven to come to his aid and slaughter the enemy in a glorious rout of good over evil, light over darkness? Now that would have made a great movie. Surely the people who killed this innocent man for political reasons were no less evil, vicious and ruthless than our modern day terrorists. Didn't they deserve what was coming to them?

Couldn't Jesus have simply embraced the time honored course of action that all of us must live by in the "real world": *kill or be killed*. Isn't it "us" or "them"? Protect yourself and your family at all costs and never show weakness. But no, not Jesus! Instead he allows this unprovoked violence to happen to him, publicly, for all the world to see.

All his detractors, the skeptics, the haters who loved to hate, he lets them win. And then..... then, to top it all off, he forgives them and makes excuses to God for them. "Father, forgive them, they know not what they do." I don't understand.

Didn't he live in the same world we live in? Didn't he know that the only way to stop hatred and violence is to stand up to it and fight? Some people only understand force. What is all this "love your enemies" psychobabble? How can anyone expect to face the world's problems with that kind of softheaded thinking? That is just not realistic.

I guess he is lucky God bailed him out on Sunday and resurrected him or he would go down as one of history's great losers. I can read the headlines now: "Rising political leader lacks killer instinct;" "Charismatic, renaissance man chokes, retreats as the pressure mounts;" "Miracle worker shown to be a fraud and a coward."

Good Friday is just embarrassing and impractical in the real world. Isn't it?

Christian poet and lyricist, Michael Card, in his song *God's Own Fool*, writes:

> *It seems I've imagined him all of my life*
> *as the wisest of all of mankind.*
> *But if God's holy wisdom is foolish to men,*
> *he must have seemed out of his mind.*

Paul said it like this: "The cross is foolishness to those who are perishing, but to us who are being saved it is the power of God." (1 Corinthians 1:18)

According to Paul, the Jews and the Gentiles didn't

like Good Friday either. For them, to die like Jesus was a sign of weakness and defeat. Still, Paul insisted that the *power* and *wisdom* of God are to be found on Good Friday and not on Easter Sunday.

I don't get it.

Are we really expected to naively believe that love is stronger than physical force, that to give in for the good of another takes more strength than to fight? Is it realistic to believe that to follow this way of Jesus would really change people's hearts and bring peace to our families, our cities and our world?

Could we honestly be expected to stop wars through caring for our enemies as if they were part of our family even when they hurt us? Are we supposed to not retaliate and simply resist with the truth as opposed to real weapons, preferring to believe that history is in the hands of a loving God?

I don't know .... I just don't know.

I'm glad Easter is in a few days so I don't have to face Jesus on the cross anymore. I prefer belonging to the church for winners. He makes me too uncomfortable.

Tips for Everyday Faith

Do you have an illustrated bible, a crucifix or a rosary? Spend some time staring at the crucified Christ this week and ask him what he was trying to say to us. Let him teach you about the love in the heart of God and the plan the Lord has for us to live in the peace of the Kingdom of God.

Is the President the AntiChrist?

My mother thinks so. Her source of information? A woman from her parish prayer group told her that it's in the Bible. I wish I could say that my mother and her parish friend are alone in these types of pronouncements but unfortunately they are not.

Every four years we endure a Presidential election with all its negative ads and mudslinging sound bytes. Inevitably, whoever wins, I am not satisfied. I cannot be. No candidate (and I even study the Third Party options) matches our vision as Catholics. I am "politically homeless," to adopt a phrase from John Carr, a veteran policy analyst for the U.S. Bishops.

The main candidates speak to certain issues, some of which I believe are non-negotiable. But once I step past those important points of agreement, I find myself longing for more. Why couldn't someone espouse a comprehensive ethic of life *and* do justice to the other issues that we hold dear as Catholics?

The economy, the need for alternative energy sources, the environment, war, trade issues, health care, immigration, education, genocides and various human rights issues are all in desperate need of attention, even if they do not trump abortion.

I suppose that whatever happens on Election Day, many people are disappointed.

But there can be a silver lining to this. For decades, many people have chosen not to engage in our country's political process. I can remember recent Presidential elections when less than 50% of the electorate bothered to cast their ballot. Whether that stems from laziness, apathy or a sense that their vote doesn't matter, it appears people nowadays are getting more engaged.

Inside our Catholic community, a surge of interest and involvement is also spiking. Some Catholics—faithful citizens, social justice advocates, pro-life activists and political junkies—have been engaged for decades. But younger Catholics, black churches and those who have lost confidence in the government have stayed away.

The recent elections have been different. Energy levels were way up, even to the point of borderline hysterics. My hope is that people don't lose steam after the election is over. Political responsibility requires more than a periodic trip to the voting booth. Our system works best when politicians hear from us and not just the lobbyists. If we stay on top of our elected officials and avoid the trap of feeling like we are stuck with results of the election, we can profoundly influence the governance of this country. In other words, our job as Catholics only begins with voting.

The U.S. Catholic Bishops, Pope John Paul II and Pope Benedict XVI all clearly teach that we are to bring our Catholic voice to the political and social questions of the day.

Do we not believe that Christ has the answers to our deepest personal and national questions? Shouldn't then our representatives in Washington D.C. and in our state legislatures benefit from Catholic wisdom on social issues? Why not stay engaged for the long haul, even if the rest of the country moves onto the next national obsession? Insist that you be heard beyond election week so that little by little Christ's vision influences every decision made in this country regardless of the issue.

Most of all, pray and fast. These spiritual weapons are the most powerful tools we have to contribute to the wellbeing of our country.

Tips for Everyday Faith

If you have friends or family members with whom you locked horns over politics, seek them out and reconcile with them. Ask for forgiveness for any harsh words you spoke or for not always respecting their opinions. If they respond in kind, forgive them for how they may have offended or hurt you. We are, after all, brothers and sisters in Christ, not to mention fellow Americans. We need each other to move forward as a people.

http://actioncenter.crs.org

Looking for a way to influence our politics, this site from *Catholic Relief Services* allows you to sign up to receive emails about specific issues as they come up for a vote. The emails allow you to sign petitions, write letters or make timely phone calls to your elected officials. If this site doesn't match your political interests, search for the right one for you.

Showing Up

I walked around my house yesterday after work. The grass is crispy, the bushes are wilting and our new baby fig tree is dying for a drink. Time for a little extra care and attention.

My spirit can look a lot like my yard at times when I neglect it or when I go through a spiritual drought. In both cases, the antidote is the same: lots of life giving water (John 4:10-15) and some solid spiritual nourishment (John 6:54-56; Colossians 3:16; 1 Timothy 4:6).

Luckily, these two items are not hard to come by. The Church, Scripture and the extended Catholic community make access to Christ's teachings and Christ's presence abundantly available. So why the drought? Why do our spiritual gardens wilt?

Quite simply, the answer is neglect. Like Jesus explained in the Parable of the Sower (Matthew 13:1-23; Mark 4:1-25; Luke 8:4-18), there are many threats to our soul's wellbeing. But for most of us, the reason we often feel spiritually dry is that we give very little care and attention to our inner life with God. Life is so busy, when we finally get around to being quiet for a few moments at the end of the day, we often fall asleep.

I have been telling myself for months that I need set aside some time for prayer. But do I do it? Nope. One-on-one time with God, despite my best intentions, always seems to get squeezed off the priority list.

Many times my reasons are legitimate. I have to work, take care of the children or do something for my wife. But, when I get real honest, I must admit that I put less important things in front of prayer time too, including: watching a movie or sports on TV; wasting time on the internet; mindless reading; doing home projects that can wait; shopping for stuff we don't really need and worrying about things I can't control.

Prayer can also sometimes seem like a waste of time. I know, I know. Of course it isn't a waste of time. But I'm so results driven, it is hard to overcome the mindset that I'm wasting time when I sit somewhere in silence. Where's the payoff?

I want to feel Christ's presence, hear the Holy Spirit talking to me, get a direct and immediate answer to a request or at least read through a book in the Bible. Something, anything so that I can convince myself that I am being productive. I need to see results.

Centuries of saints and holy people, however, insist that prayer doesn't work this way. Time spent with God slowly, steadily, imperceptibly changes us, unmasks us, and transforms us. It is like the effects of the sun on an overcast day. We don't always feel the sun's rays but when we go inside, we are burnt. (A teenager once told me that she liked Eucharistic Adoration because she was getting a Son tan.)

Our job is to show up. *We are responsible for the quantity of prayer. God is responsible for the quality.* If we have visions, hear a direct word from the Lord or sense Christ's presence with us, that is up to God. We can only control one thing. Are we there? Are we making time for God to enter more profoundly into our lives and change us? Do we show up?

Lately, I jumped on board again with the *40 Days for Life* campaign which asks people to pray, fast and stand out in front of the local abortion clinic in peaceful protest. I signed up for the 6 a.m. shift, Monday through Friday. People may assume that this indicates I am strongly pro-life. I am. But the truth is that 6 a.m. is a great time for me to pray, before the responsibilities of the day come crashing down on me.

So every morning now I get my tired bones out of bed

and head out in the dark. I'm showing up and God is working on me. I don't know how God is changing me yet, but I trust God's promise. "What I do now you will not always understand but in time, you will see clearly." (John 13:7)

Tips for Everyday Faith

For prayer to be consistent, we often need a spiritual practice to anchor or focus us. Some ideas include the rosary, reflecting on the Mass readings for the day (*magnificat.com, wau.org*), repeating a prayerful word or phrase, using daily devotionals (*livingfaith.org, odb.org*), the liturgy of the hours, writing in a journal, taking a prayer walk, or spiritual reading. All these practices create a prayer pattern that helps create a rhythm to our prayer. They also transition our minds from distraction to attentiveness so that we can be present to God.

www.catholicdoors.com/prayers

This site lists over 3,000 prayers including many traditional prayers, saint's prayers and prayers for all occasions.

A Baby Named Adam

Two times in my life I stared abortion right in the face. Both confrontations revealed to me how sad and terrible the choice was for those involved.

The first time I was 19 years old, preparing for a college semester abroad in Spain. A week before the trip, I visited a friend who had just returned from Spain. I went to ask her for some packing tips. Instead, she revealed to me that she thought she was pregnant. Looking into Jill's eyes, I could tell she didn't need a lecture about sexual morality. What she needed was comfort and support. She was petrified and feeling very alone.

I suggested that she tell her parents. But Jill balked. All her life she had heard her father's warnings. "If you ever come home pregnant, I'll disown you, kill the boy who did that to you and then kill myself." She knew he wasn't bluffing.

What about the guy, I asked. Again she dismissed the idea saying that her boyfriend still lived in Spain and she did not plan to tell him because they broke up the day before she returned to the U.S.

I offered some feeble words of comfort. Then a (sincere but naïve) thought dawned on me. Maybe I could take on the role of the father. Perhaps I could even marry her, after all we were great friends. When I told Jill my idea, the dark clouds of fear and isolation began to give way. Relief and gratitude began to take hold as she realized she would not have to face this crisis alone. Tears covered her cheeks and for the moment, it seemed like things would be alright.

On my drive home, the implications of my surrogate fatherhood proposal began to sink in. I would obviously not be going to Spain. Probably, I should quit school in Boston, move closer to Jill and start looking for a decent job. As I mulled over these practical considerations, an undetected thought floated into my consciousness. "Maybe she should just have an abortion. Who would know? We could both be back at school by the start of the new semester." Shocked and appalled, I realized the allure abortion held for those facing situations like this. It all seemed so reasonable. Abortion could "make it all go away."

I was ashamed that I even thought such a thing. I was a staunch pro-life advocate. But there it was, so easy, so quick, so tempting. I drove the thought from my mind but now I knew. This is how it happens. This is how good people end up killing their babies. Jill called me later that week and gleefully announced that her pregnancy test came back negative. I was on a plane headed to Spain the next day, relieved as well as chastened.

My second personal encounter with abortion happened years later on a retreat. A young man, Tyler, had abruptly left the chapel during a penance service. I walked out after him and listened as he explained how God could never forgive him for what he had done.

As he spoke, a subtle whisper in my mind said: "He got a girl pregnant and she aborted the baby." Unnerved by this information, which I assumed came from God, I wondered what to do. Clearly, Tyler despaired of God's love for him. He was torturing himself but too ashamed to tell anyone.

Tentatively, I asked him if he got a girl pregnant. Shocked by my question, he quickly melted into a pool of tears. His slumping shoulders heaved with each sob as he told me that I was right and that his baby, he whispered, was dead.

He didn't want the abortion but what could he do? It was her body, after all, he said. Now he and his girlfriend weren't even talking anymore.

"Deep down, I knew it was wrong, the sex and everything," he explained. "Then she tells me she is pregnant and plans to have an abortion. I didn't say a thing."

Another wave of tears crashed down over him. "I didn't say anything. I let her kill our baby. What kind of father am I? I didn't even defend my own child."

After some time I suggested that, if he knew the gender of the baby—he did, it was a boy—that he give his child a name and begin to talk to him. Tell him what happened and how he was so sorry. Ask his son to forgive him. Then find a place in the woods and create a burial site to lay his baby to rest, in his heart.

Two weeks later I bumped into Tyler and asked him how he was doing. He told me he named the baby, Adam, and buried him behind his house where he could visit him often. Tyler also told me that he had made an appointment to go to confession. I assured him that God was with him and his son. He nodded, as if to say, I hope so.

I left him with one more task. "Pray for your ex-girlfriend. I'm sure she is hurting too."

Abortion kills on many levels. A baby dies at the hand of its parents. Mothers and fathers take part in the murder of their own children. Consciences are silenced, souls are mortally wounded, and paths to God are blocked.

Is there any hope? Jesus offers this word of truth: "The thief comes only to steal, kill and destroy. But I have come that you might have life..." (John 10:10). So like the Moses and the Israelites in the desert (Deuteronomy 30:19), God sets before us the blessing and the curse, life and death. I pray we choose life.

I'm a Good Person.
Why Do I Need to Go to Church?

Have you ever heard this type of reasoning before? I have. In fact, there was a time that I thought like this.

The logic is as follows: "if I am a decent human being—don't steal, don't kill, don't cheat on my taxes or my significant other—why do I need the church? I'm no worse than most people who go to church and from what I have seen, in some ways I may be better."

How do we respond? After all, we cannot deny that regular churchgoers and leaders sometimes do embarrassingly immoral things, myself included. That has always been true, and as long as the church includes human beings, it will continue to be true.

Moreover, it is true that many non-churchgoers are decent people, fine citizens and exemplars of basic moral living. They live out the Golden Rule and treat others with dignity and respect. So then what benefit comes from active engagement in a community of disciples of Jesus?

To answer this, we need to look at the difference between secular and Christian morality. All civilized societies throughout history required a shared set of ethics to function. Community members agreed to abide by these expectations and those who deviated were sanctioned, i.e. put in jail. Societies that do not establish a common moral code descend into chaos. The ancient Greeks and Romans thrived in part because of the great value they placed on the cardinal virtues of prudence, temperance, justice and fortitude. In other words, ethics and virtue did not originate with Christianity. In fact, all the major world religions and great civilizations have taught morality.

Christianity, however, uniquely builds upon this

basic human instinct for moral structure. To this innate sense of right and wrong, Christ adds the Holy Spirit and that changes the equation. The Spirit of God ups the ante. Human nature can take us only so far. But God's Spirit invites us into a life of supernatural virtue. The grace of the Holy Spirit takes our basic humanity and charges it with the very life of God.

The result is that we go from being willing to die for our country, like the Romans, to being willing to die for our enemies, like Jesus. We move from being people who are worried about meeting our needs to people who live generously so that those around us are taken care of, even those who do not deserve it. We change our perspective from "what will this cost me and my family" to "how can I cooperate with God, knowing that God will provide for whatever we need." (Matthew 6:33)

Consider the saints. Were they exceptions to the rule, extraordinary human beings with the "holiness gene" given to a few in history; spiritual equivalents to singular athletes like Nadia Comaneci, Michael Phelps or Michael Jordan? Hardly. Saints are normal people who cooperate with the Holy Spirit. They hear Jesus and take him at his Word: "you will do greater things than me" (John 14:12), and "you will receive power when the Holy Spirit comes upon you, and you will be my witnesses ... to the ends of the earth." (Acts 1:8).

As a Catholic community, we believe so deeply in God's gift of the Holy Spirit that we sacramentalize this experience of being born anew into the life of God. Baptism and Confirmation take the basic raw material of our humanity and infuse it with so much supernatural power, Paul says we are a "new creation", the old has passed away (2 Corinthians 5:17). He calls *all* the baptized *saints*. (Rom 15:25, 2 Corinthians 1:1, Ephesians 1:1, Phil 1:1).

The early church described this reality as *divinization*, which means that we become Christ to the world today because his Spirit lives within us.

If non-believers and non-practicing Catholics can look at us and say "my life is no different than yours," we need to seriously examine how we are living. Are we allowing the Spirit of God to lead us beyond our basic human nature into the graced life of Christ? Are our hearts stretching to include more and more people into the circle of those for whom we care: immigrants, the poor, our enemies, the undeserving, criminals, unborn children, the addicted, crooked politicians, public sinners, those who have hurt us and those who hate us? These are the marks of Christian morality and they stand in dramatic contrast to the morality of secular society. Didn't Jesus say: *If you love those who love you, what credit is that to you? For even sinners love those who love them.* (Luke 6:32)

If this description of Christian morality sounds unattainable and impossible to live, you are starting to get the picture. Not one of us, by our own strength, can will ourselves to be this sacrificial, this heroic in our everyday life. We need God's Spirit. We need the Christian community to support us and the Church to sustain us in prayer and sacrament. We need to be on our knees regularly begging God for the faith and the courage to be what he created us to be—saints, martyrs, witnesses and ambassadors. Our lives must point to a reality so superior to the good things of life that we live unattached to all this world has to offer.

Why do we need to go to Church? Simply put, the life of profound meaning and relevance God desires for us thrives best in the community that uses Jesus on the cross as its measuring stick for morality.

The Not So Distant God

I visited my parents in their retirement community over the Thanksgiving holiday. The drive is about eight hours. With two small children under five years old and a newborn, we need a strategy for a trip of this length. After some painful back seat brawls and a series of meltdowns, we've taken to driving through the night while the kiddies are fast asleep.

Sure I am delirious with exhaustion when we arrive at Grandma and Grandpa's place, but at least my nerves aren't shot.

To be quite honest, I don't mind it at all. Overnight trips seem to have a mystical quality for me.

I remember when I flew to Rome for a friend's ordination years ago. I settled in after the meal and planned to sleep the flight away. Instead, I looked out the plane window at the dome in the sky, saturated as it was with fiery stars and far off planets. I could swear they were within arm's reach if I could just stretch out my hand through the plane window.

My mind flooded with scriptures from the psalms and the Genesis creation stories. How marvelous are your works O Lord, how perfect are your ways, I thought to myself. The constellations and the impenetrable black sky curved on all horizons. Impossible, majestic, sublime. Artistic genius on a universal scale. I marveled as my heart filled with wonder and awe.

A praise song came to mind—"Praise be to the God and Father of our Lord Jesus Christ, through His great mercy He has given us new life." Without warning or expectation, I found myself being transported to another place. I hadn't left my seat on the plane but somehow I was not there anymore. My spirit slipped through that plexi-glass window and into the company of God and His angels, floating among the stars in the endless sky.

I was not asleep and yet I felt profoundly at rest. My deepest self surrendered to this transcendent communion with God and all of creation. I did not move nor did I notice the details of my body anymore. My need to understand what was happening submitted to the experience of peace and at-one-ness with everything and everyone. Time and space collapsed and I knew I was being given a taste of what theologians and saints describe as the *mysterium tremendum*—the mystery of God's presence.

When I returned to myself, four hours had passed and we were beginning our descent into Italy. Soon the sun would peak up over the horizon and another day would begin. But how could I forget that timeless moment with the Lord over the Atlantic?

Over the years, popular "spiritual" authors like Eckhart Tolle and James Redfield have chronicled their personal journeys to enlightenment. Appealing to the New Age (i.e. not comfortable with traditional religion) market, these authors present spiritual programs that mirror the mystical tradition of the Catholic tradition, albeit in diminished forms.

They do present one intriguing truth that continues to attract people: they describe an encounter with the Divine. The God of the universe, the creator of all things, the tremendous mystery that is above all things and in all things, is somehow accessible to normal people like you and me. Open yourself and submit your mind and soul to this divine energy and you may experience a profound communion with all that is, they tell us.

This is nothing new for us Catholics. Minus the heresies and distortions, the Catholic faith confronts us with the same truth: God is with us. God can be known and wants to be known.

Catholicism insists that God is a God of relationship.

More surprisingly, God wants a relationship with us.

To that end, God provides us with His words in Scripture, His example in Christ and the saints, His abiding Spirit in our souls and in the Church and His very life in the Eucharist. He is inviting us into a mystical Holy Communion.

Our faith tells us that the Almighty God, the creator of the stars in the heavens, desires for you to know Him, personally, in the everyday circumstances of your life. So great is God's desire for you, He will even meet you on a plane or driving in your car at night.

God is not so distant, so unknown.

New spiritual programs will come and go but the Catholic way has been tried and been proven to be trustworthy. All that we need to encounter the Lord has been given to us. For unto us a child is born. Emmanuel, God with us. Christ the Lord.

Love has come for the world to know. Perhaps this evening, dim the lights, quiet your mind and rest in His presence. You never know where God might take you. So sit back, relax and enjoy the flight.

God Never Blinks

One of the great benefits of being a Christian is to remind people that God never blinks. He doesn't get distracted or take his eyes off us, ever. In fact, if God stopped thinking about us for one minute, we wouldn't be in hell, we would disappear.

For me, as a baptized Catholic called to work in lay ministry, I have the privilege and the responsibility of representing God and His Church to others.

Take for example this past weekend. My wife and I visited a friend, Laura, who discovered her faith through a mission trip I led to Mexico nine years ago. When we listened to all that she has endured since we last saw her, our hearts broke.

Over the past few years, Laura has nursed a profoundly sick child. Her sister just died of an overdose. Her father was in jail. And her marriage collapsed—the divorce was finalized last Friday. She currently goes to counseling with her seven-year old daughter so they can cope with the trauma of the divorce and the younger brother's illness.

Honestly, I didn't know how Laura wasn't sitting in the corner of her living room crying her eyes out.

I stood up at one point and simply hugged her and told her she was "beautiful and a walking miracle." She looked at me like I had just given her oxygen after months of holding her breath.

As my wife and I left, Laura walked us to our car where we prayed over her, reminding her of God's faithfulness. When we finished, Laura said: "Once before when we were in Mexico together, I felt like God reached out to me when I felt lost. I think that is happening again right now." We left knowing she was in good hands.

A few hours later, we attended a wedding of a young woman, Cathy, who is a spiritual powerhouse. Evidently, her new husband is one too.

The wedding Mass was packed with people--young and old—we knew from my ministry here years ago. With so much faith in the building, the ceremony felt more like a revival than the typical wedding. The priest even commented that he was so inspired by the devotion and Christian commitment of the couple that it made him want to be a better priest. I'm sure many of the couples in the pews, my wife and I included, felt the same way about our vocations.

At the reception, Cathy, her family and several of the guests told us how they missed us at the parish and how much it meant that we were there. One former youth group member in the bridal party mentioned that she cried coming up the aisle when she saw us.

I knew these people weren't reacting to us this way. We represented the presence of Christ to them because of how we had experienced the love of God together in the years I ministered there. So when they looked at us, they were reminded of how good the Lord had been and still is.

Later at the reception, in a quiet moment, I told my wife that my heart could not absorb it all. It was just too overwhelming. God had taken us in those few hours from the depths of despair to the heights of joy-filled revelry. From sadness and sickness, to sacrament and celebration. And God never blinked.

Through every moment, high and low, God was with us and with our friends. In the morning, we joined Job on the dung hill of asking God "why?" (Job 2-3) And in the afternoon, we danced with Jesus at the Wedding of Cana. (John 2:1-11) But one thing remained clear throughout the day. The God of our faith never slumbers nor sleeps. (Psalm 121:4) He is with us when we are walking on water. And He is just as present when we start to sink. (Matthew 14:22-33) Maybe more.

Tips for Everyday Faith

Read a good book about how faithful God is through good times and bad. Try "God Never Blinks" by Regina Brett. The author recounts her life and the lessons she learned as a teenage drunk, an unwed mother, a cancer survivor and now a successful writer.

The End of the World

Not unlike many other people, I love a good Armageddon movie or book. There is something about the fragility of our existence on this earth that lends itself to this type of tale.

Even before the current blockbuster hit the theaters, many apocalyptic possibilities had been explored in books and the movies including alien invasions, rogue asteroids, nuclear annihilations, global environmental disasters, unstoppable diseases and computers/ robots/androids/transformers/micro-technologies gone wild.

The bible offers a few end-of-the-world scenarios as well with some pretty scary references to wars, earthquakes, stars falling, people dying from fear and angels swooping in to round up "the elect." (Mk 13, Luke 21)

Born again Christians take these verses, along with others (Matthew 24:40-41, John 14:1-3, 1 Thessalonians 4:13-18) to support their Rapture/Tribulation theology of the Second Coming of Christ. Their ideas, popularized in the *Left Behind* series, describe a moment when those who are saved will be taken up to heaven by Christ (and the angels), thus escaping the time of tribulation and judgment.

Those who are left behind? Look out! These poor souls will be left to the devil and the worst kind of evil in this world. If they survive that, some born again preachers like TV evangelist John Hagee say they will face a Jesus that acts more like Rambo than the Christ of the gospels. "The first time he came to earth, Jesus was the Lamb of God, led in silence to the slaughter. The next time he comes, he will be the Lion of Judah who will trample his enemies until their blood stains his garments, and he shall rule with a rod of iron."

But do Catholics believe the same thing about the end times?

We certainly expect and pray for Jesus to come again. At every Mass we unequivocally state in the Nicene Creed that Christ "will come again in glory to judge the living and the dead." Then we proclaim the mystery of faith (pre-changes), saying things like: "Christ has died, Christ is risen, Christ will come again" or "Dying you destroyed our death. Rising you restored our life. Lord Jesus come in glory." Finally, we pray during the Our Father that "thy kingdom come."

So we do believe Christ will come again as the scriptures describe. But we understand these bible readings as part of the larger message of the gospel Jesus preached.

Christ preached and embodied love for your enemies, forgiveness for the unforgivable and mercy for those beaten down by life's cruelties. He spoke of our Father who created us to live in right relationships with one another.

This message wasn't just a last attempt to save a few before the Father took out His vengeance against the human race. We believe that the gospel tells us about the fundamental nature of God in Godself. God is love (1 John 4:8) and whoever sees Christ, sees what the Father is really like (John 14:9).

The second coming is not something we fear. Rather, we welcome the return of Christ as a fulfillment of our great hope that everything that is still rotten in this world will be made right.

As Pope Benedict says in *Spes Salvi*, part of that making right will involve some justice for those who have rebelled against God. But isn't that something we all want? Aren't we sickened when criminals, dictators or terrorists get away with evil acts? Don't we long for a day of reckoning when people will have to pay for the atrocities they have committed? Would we really want a God who would let those things go without punishment?

Unlike our fundamentalist friends, Catholics are not restricted by a literal reading of every bible verse. We don't have to explain literally how the moon could turn to blood or the God of love in chapters 1-23 could turn so merciless by chapter 24. Instead, we recognize the larger message of these apocalyptic texts.

The bible writers, including St. Paul, wanted to remind their readers that God is in control. That is the bottom line. For the first century Christians who were being murdered en masse by Nero and Diocletian, these words brought them great comfort. But when we understand them correctly, they still are a source of tremendous encouragement for us today.

When you are diagnosed with cancer, lose your job, have a sudden death in the family, experience a painful end to a relationship or simply feel alone, the same God who has blessed you in your successes has not abandoned you in your sufferings.

In fact, the Greek word used for the Second Coming in the New Testament is *parousia*, which can be translated to mean "to be present" or "at your side." In other words, Christ has never left you. He is still here, standing by your side. Our job as Catholic Christians is to live in such a way as to make His presence felt to all those around us.

As Christ tells us, no one will know the day or the hour when Christ will fully reveal His presence to us again in His Second Coming. But until that day, we live in His love, knowing that God is with us no matter what, even if the sun goes dark and the stars fall from the sky. Those things are not a problem when the light of the world lives in your heart. (John 8:12)

The Catholic Church
and the "Real World"

When I was in college, so many of my friends and colleagues attacked the Catholic Church as being out of touch, frozen in some medieval world where church affairs dominated everyday life. "What the Church says is irrelevant to the real world," those critics used to say. Their voices were strong and still are.

Fortunately, as the years have passed, I've chosen to investigate the Church's relevance for myself. I discovered that far from being out of touch and irrelevant, our Church is deeply involved in the great struggles of our day. Any examination of the Church's role in the fall of the Soviet Union, the anti-capital punishment movement, the call for forgiveness of Third World debts, not to mention the ongoing pro-life battle, provides clear evidence that the Church is a leading moral voice in our world.

The foundation for the Church's prophetic involvement in world affairs can be found in the seven principles of Catholic Social Teaching (www.osjspm.org): *Life & Dignity of the Human Person; Community & the Common Good; Rights & Responsibilities; Option for the Poor; Dignity of Work; Solidarity; and Care for God's Creation.* These seven principles provide the philosophical and theological underpinnings for the Church to "stick its nose" into the most controversial issues. For example:

Principle #1--Life & Dignity of the Human Person

"Keep your rosary off my uterus" reads an abortion rights sign at a Planned Parenthood rally. But we cannot because the *Life and Dignity of the Human Person* demands that the followers of Jesus defend life at all its stages from conception to natural death. Moreover, life requires more than breath. It demands dignity. That means common practices like slavery, child labor, sweatshops, pornography, sexual exploitation or any degradation of our God given dignity cannot be tolerated. Nothing but the full flourishing of each human person satisfies the call of Principle #1. Even if some think these issues are none of the Church's business, Christ compels us to *make it our business*. After all, if the Kingdom of God is to be built, we, who are the Body of Christ in the world today, are God's main work force.

Principle #4—Option for the Poor

"I have some money to invest and I want to get into the stock market. Any suggestions?" In today's world, this is not an uncommon conversation, especially for singles or young professional couples without children. The *Option for the Poor* principle pushes us to include Jesus in this very secular consideration. Jesus tells us in Matt 25:31ff that what we do to the least in our human community, we do to Him. In other words, when we chose to invest only in our own interests and not in the concerns of the hurting people in the world, we turn our backs on the suffering Jesus. When we save our money in banks instead of in the stomachs of starving children, we ignore the hungry Jesus. Matt 25 says we will have to explain that to Jesus on Judgment Day. That's serious business! That is a challenge we cringe to hear and want to reject as extreme, overwhelming or simply irresponsible. But the Church won't let us dismiss the Lord that easily. In the *Option for the Poor,* our Church challenges us to consider the poor when we allocate our resources. Who are the people who need these resources the most? Who is most hurting? Can we not somehow share our abundance with them? This moral criteria applies to each one of us individually, to our businesses, to the church and to our nation. And it is not just about money. How do we opt for the poor with our time, our career decisions, how we socialize, how we vote and with whom we associate?

Are you starting to see how relevant our Church is in the "real world"? My critical friends have it much easier than faithful Catholics. They just ignore Jesus and His Church. Taking our tradition seriously is to feel the radical call of the gospel. Thankfully, when we see the impossible demands of Christ, we will realize how much we need Him, and in needing Him we may discover how radically He loves us in our successes and even more resolutely in our struggles to live His magnificent gospel.

The mission is much bigger than doing something for the church or joining a bible class. The mission is the building the kingdom of God right here, right now in our towns, jobs, schools, homes, families and churches. It is imminently relevant to our everyday lives. In fact, it is a little scary. After all, they killed Jesus for trying this once before.

Check out these websites for more info and ideas: www.usccb.org/sdwp or www.aquinasfunds.com——go to the *Who Are We* link to read their commitment to "Catholic Value Investing."

Sharing the Faith

Many Catholics feel intimidated to share their faith. Jesus never intended for the Great Commission (Matt 28:19-20) to be an impossible burden. Rather, God intended us to witness for Christ as a natural outcome of living for him.

Here are a few tips for sharing Christ with others.

You can't give what you don't have. Faith is more often caught than taught. That means we have to be carrying the bug so we can pass it on to others. If our life is filled with God and the things God is doing, it will be much easier to speak to others about the joys of knowing Christ.

When faith is something we intellectually accept but rarely do anything with, of course we are intimated to talk about Christ. We are speaking of a subject about which we know very little. Or worse, we are hypocrites, telling others to do what we don't do ourselves.

Once a woman approached Gandhi to ask him to tell her son to cut back on sugar. Gandhi agreed but sent her home with an invitation to return in a month. When she returned with her son, Gandhi instructed him to limit his sugar. The woman, confused by the month delay, asked Gandhi about it. He said: "I couldn't tell the boy what I wasn't living myself. So I needed a month to break my own addiction to sugar."

Prepare your testimony. St. Peter in his first letter writes: "Be prepared to give an answer to everyone who asks you to explain the hope that is within you." (1 Peter 3:15) In other words, we need to be ready when God opens the door for us to speak about Him in our lives.

In order to do this well, it helps to take some time and reflect on our personal story. What was my life like before God was in the center? What happened that caused the change? What is different since then?

If you have this testimony ready, God will give you the chance to share it. Maybe a friend, spouse or child will ask you why you go to church or why your faith is so important to you. Be ready and then pray to the Holy Spirit for opportunities, for the courage to speak and for the right words to touch the heart of the person listening.

Offer to pray with people. Most decent people will listen and help when there is a crisis. But, as Catholics, we can do even more. We can invite God into the situation through prayer.

This can come in the normal way by offering to pray for the person. But what if you reached out to that hurting person and prayed with them right there. Wouldn't it be nice, if you were struggling, to hear someone speak to God on your behalf out loud, right when you needed God's help the most?

It can be intimidating to be so spontaneous. But it shouldn't be. If we are talking to Jesus all the time, why should we be so shy to talk to Him with a friend or family member in distress? Our prayers don't have to be Shakespeare. Just pray from your heart.

Intimate, personal prayer is one of the great treasures given to us by Christ. Why not use it to bless others who are sick, scared, worried, lonely or overwhelmed? We are Christ's ambassadors, after all. (2 Corinthians 5:20).

Twice this past month, friends who were visiting challenged me to be more free with my prayer. One woman, before saying goodnight for the evening said, "let's have a psalm" and proceeded to read Psalm 121 for all of us to pray. Another friend before leaving after dinner, gathered my family into a circle, children included, and offered a prayer for us all. Beautiful. Such a gift.

Evangelization is a big word and a big task, one that many would like to leave to the priests. Too bad a lot of the people who need Christ don't go to church or know a priest. They do, however, know us. We work with them, live next to them or go to school with them. Why not share the gift Christ has given us?

Sharing your faith or offering a prayer is not the same as thumping someone with a bible or coercing them to attend your church. It is an act of love and that is evangelization. After all, God is love. (1 John 4:8)

Missionary in Everyday Life

Fred Tiemann is 43 years old, newly married, a baby on the way, native of Minnesota, resident of West Mobile, lawyer, Roman Catholic, daily communicant—*missionary in his everyday life.*

Like many Catholics these days, Fred Tiemann lives his faith in the most secular of settings.

"I used to be an accountant", recalls Tiemann, "but as I grew in my Catholic faith and my relationship with God, I felt drawn to become a lawyer."

Tiemann responded to God's call by attending law school at the University of Notre Dame. Like many of his classmates, he was idealistic about the legal profession and his ability to effect positive change as a lawyer.

"I knew I didn't want to work in the corporate world where the emphasis can often be on how many billable hours you rack up," he explains. "So I chose to work for people charged with a crime who needed someone to make sure their rights were respected."

Specifically, Tiemann took a position as a Federal Public Defender. His exact role is to provide legal counsel for clients who cannot afford an attorney.

"I have a choice as to what I do with my abilities and my education. I choose to serve the poor," he states. "All my clients are poor."

After years as a Public Defender, Tiemann knows not to idealize "the poor," a trap into which many social activists fall. The clients he serves are often both a victim and a victimizer. But Tiemann feels that his faith compels him to be Christ to them despite their behavior.

"Many of my clients committed the crimes," he admits. "But that doesn't mean that they don't have rights or that they can be run over by the legal system. Someone has to fight for them.

"Honestly, I know many people would prefer if my clients disappeared from Mobile; maybe move, die or be put in jail for good. But I doubt that is how God thinks about them. They still are his children as much as we are."

That kind of thinking is what sustains Tiemann in a job that requires long hours and little immediate gratification. More than winning cases, Tiemann sees his job as a place where he lives out his discipleship.

"When I stand with my clients through the legal process and show them that someone cares about them, I practice my profession and I serve God at the same time," he says.

That doesn't mean being a Public Defender doesn't have its problems.

"It is very frustrating at times," he says. "I wish I could smack some sense into some of my clients and say 'Stop smoking crack!' It would be easy to give up and just lock them up for good. But we believe that all people are capable of conversion. We also believe that we have an intrinsic dignity that comes from being made in God's image. If that doesn't make a difference in how I treat my clients, I'm just wasting my time at church."

Does that mean that people shouldn't go to jail?

Tiemann continues: "The point I'm making isn't about whether they should go to jail or not. The point is how do I treat these vulnerable people. Is it anything like how Jesus treated the people he met who were accused of a crime?"

Tiemann highlights two significant influences in how he lives his faith: Catholic Social Teaching and the insights of modern saints like Mother Teresa and Archbishop Oscar Romero.

"For me, how I treat these people is how I treat Christ," he explains. "Matthew 25 is clear—Jesus is there in the least of our brothers and sisters. And let me tell you, you can't get any lower in our society than to be poor, drug addicted or a convicted criminal. It may sound pious but its true—that is Jesus and I have a chance to love him and serve him."

Being Uncomfortable

One of the great blessings of living in the U.S. is that Americans are a "can do" people. When confronted with a challenge, we face it head on and conquer it. There is nothing we can't do.

In many ways, this attitude is what makes our nation great. Perhaps our most significant export over the past 300 years has been our spirit of ingenuity.

This leads to development, innovation and growth. More is always better and better is never good enough, not if we can upgrade to "best." Driven by this engine of endless improvement, the economy hums along and everyone's lifestyle ticks upward and onward. Sounds fantastic except....

What about when things cannot be so easily fixed or when the economy tanks? What happens when a people who are not used to doing without are confronted with the prospect of scarcity?

Think about how most of us live. When we are sick, we expect pills or doctors to quickly cure us. When something is broken, we get it fixed or, more often nowadays, we simply replace the annoying item. And while we are at the store, we might as well upgrade (think cellphone, car, flat screen TV, computer, etc.)

If we are hungry, we access our overstocked pantries and fridges for a snack or a meal or a reason to go out for food. If we are lazy, frustrated or bored, we eat, surf the web or watch TV. If we get cold or hot, we adjust the temperature in our home or office. (Right now I have a space heater under my desk to make sure my delicate ankles don't suffer in this unrelenting cold. By the way, the office heat is set to 68 degrees.)

When are we uncomfortable? Practically never. We

are Americans. If we have a problem, we fix it.

Is it any wonder that we struggle with problems that are not so easily solved? How many of us are stunned that our spouses can't get their act together and make the changes we have "lovingly" recommended? What about our children? Why won't they listen and obey our sage direction? Why are our aging parents so difficult? Let's not even bring up our co-workers, neighbors or bosses.

How do we deal with the limitations of aging and sickness that lead to long term disability, chronic suffering and inevitable death?

The answer is that we don't. We don't deal well with these problems, hence the 50% divorce rate, the tremendous stress within the family unit, the endless discussions about quality of life issues and end of life choices.

Long suffering, inconvenience, discomfort, endless sacrifice, doing without, extended self-denial, these concepts don't fit very well into the American ethos.

Luckily for us Catholics, they fit perfectly into the gospel of Jesus Christ. In fact, Jesus celebrates the people who are not addicted to happiness, comfort and the ability to control their own realities. He says things like "happy are those who mourn, who are persecuted, who are poor, and who are insulted." (Matt 5: 3-12)

Did you ever wonder why the Beatitudes sound so bizarre to us? How are we, who are so practiced in being comfortable and expecting life problems to be solved by a trip to Walmart, how are we expected to understand the blessing of suffering? It seems like nonsense, or perhaps a level of spiritual elitism that we happily leave for the Mother Teresas of the world. "After all, I'm just trying to get by like everyone else," we think.

What is lost when we become more American than Christian is the tremendous spiritual power that comes with the knowledge of what to do when we suffer or when things don't go our way. Do we whine and complain, acting as if life owes us a carefree existence? Or do we tap into the truth of Christ on the cross and agree to turn our loss into God's gain?

Years ago in our church, people were taught to "offer it up." In other words, Catholics recognized that Jesus was inviting us to join him on the cross by turning our less than comfortable realities into a prayer for God's will to be done; a simple act of surrendering that taps into the same power that Christ unleashed on the cross.

This spirit of submission before God (notice how as Americans we bristle at that word "submission") allows us to face life's challenges with a peaceful assurance, knowing that in God's hands our suffering can be used for good.

The alternative is to waste our lives endlessly trying to avoid life's aggravations, as if we could. No life goes untouched by suffering.

By suffering for God, offering it up for others, we can accomplish untold good for people, including people we may never meet. Maybe God will use our surrendered suffering to inspire some "can do" American to find the cure for cancer.

There is so much good in this country of ours. But when the American way runs contrary to the way of Jesus, who is THE WAY, we know as Catholics that Jesus' way is the one that leads to the abundant life. If the American ethos really could give us inner joy, why are so many rich, beautiful, thin, powerful, famous, pampered people so miserable and all screwed up?

Consider this: Christ is the savior who suffered before He rose. He is the winner who lost before he made good. He is the conqueror who was humiliated and defeated before anyone even bothered to imagine that the cross was part of the plan. And Jesus is the one who tells us that the cross must be a part of our lives or there will be no resurrection and lasting joy. "Unless a grain of wheat falls to the ground and dies, it remains just a grain of wheat; but if it dies, it produces much fruit..." (John 12:24)

Happy suffering.

Tips for Everyday Faith

Become conscious of how often you are annoyed, frustrated, uncomfortable and wishing you could impose your will on a situation. This happens every day, all the time. They may not be the same as suffering with cancer but they are little deaths, deaths of our ego. Don't miss these opportunities to give yourself over to God. Trust that God is in control, even if you are not. Surrender your aggravation, your agitation, your exasperation into His loving hands. Your problem might not be solved but does it really matter anyway? Developing this habit of surrendering to God is what is important. Moreover, this little offering is how we join Jesus in moving the cosmic spiritual battle towards the victory of the Kingdom of God.

Most Catholic Adults
Really Don't Know Their Faith

I hear this statement a lot these days. Sometimes it comes after Protestants challenge us with Bible quotes and we are left unable to adequately respond. Other times the sentiment is raised in discussions about public moral questions like abortion, the *Just War Theory* or illegal immigration.

"What exactly does the Church say about voting for pro-choice politicians or starting a war in Iraq?" confused parishioners have asked.

But, by far, the place I hear this opinion the most is among people who work in professional religion. People in professional religion, with their degrees in theology and years of religious formation, are hard pressed not to come to this conclusion. Here's why: Most of us adult Catholics either went to CCD or Catholic school decades ago. Our lives now are busy with work, family, children, community and many other commitments. It has been years since we engaged in any formal religious education and honestly, when we were young, we weren't always paying attention in religion class. So it may not be totally unfair to say Catholics need a refresher course in their faith.

But let me challenge the notion that adult Catholics are ignorant of the Catholic faith.

Do you know any prayers by heart—the Our Father, the Hail Mary and maybe a bunch more depending on your style of prayer. I would bet that you could do the majority of the prayers from Mass by memory—even the priest's parts—if you could say them alongside someone else.

Do you know any parts of the Bible? The story of the

Prodigal Son, the Good Samaritan, Adam and Eve, Noah's Ark, Moses and the Exodus, the Birth of Jesus, his crucifixion, the famous "Love" passage from 1 Corinthians—*Love is patient, love is kind.* How about these: "Whatever you do to the least of my brothers and sisters, you do to me;" "For God so loved the world that He gave His only son...;" "The Lord is my shepherd;" "The Lord is my light and my salvation;" and the list goes on and on.

Catholic adults know a lot about the Catholic faith and even the Bible. Now, don't ask us to locate the line in the scriptures or in the catechism, but these lessons have become a part of our lives. Faith is the air we breathe and the foundation upon which we lean. Faith informs how we raise our kids, make moral choices and decide what new direction to take in life.

Gratefully, a hunger among adults for more Catholic education and faith formation is growing. Maybe we want to know how to respond to our Protestants friends. Perhaps we realize that our childhood understandings of Catholicism fall short in addressing the complexity of our adult worlds. Why belong to a religion if it doesn't help us answer life's ultimate questions?

So we are exploring. Some look outside the Church at other religions or spiritual movements. But I dare say that there is something about being Catholic and growing up with the Eucharist that always draws us back. Even if for years we belong to *First Baptist Evangelical Fellowship of the Church of Christ* and we love the preaching, the music, the emphasis on scripture, the community and the dynamic programming, we always miss the Eucharist. It is as if Christ is calling us home for Thanksgiving. "Come to the table where I will feed you," he says. Many return home. Some do not.

At the heart of Catholicism is something that is deeper than quoting the bible or intellectual knowledge of the faith. Yes, we do need to learn what we believe and how those beliefs translate into our everyday life. And yes, it wouldn't hurt to read and study the bible more at home and in groups. But deep down in our Catholic souls, we are part of the beautiful vision of Jesus, where God is present in the religious places and in the kitchen sinks. We are members of a community that believes that service *is* preaching and that suffering and sacrifice can bring holiness. We believe that saints and sinners are all invited to God's house for dinner and that it is God's graciousness that gives us the guts to silence the demons within us.

You see, beyond all the right words, the perfect prayers and the exact definitions of doctrines, there is love, with all its messiness and uncertainty. According to Catholicism, love changes the equation. Love moves us from "there, but for the grace of God, go I" to the heart of Christ's invitation—"there, with the grace of God, I will go." If we know this about our faith, we know everything.

Tips for Everyday Faith

The quote in the last paragraph comes from the speaker/author Paula D'Arcy. If you find yourself grieving the loss of a loved one or experiencing any major loss in your life, read her classic book, *Gift of the Red Bird.* This book was the fruit of her spiritual journey after the loss of her husband and 21 month old daughter in a drunk driving accident.

For Richer, For Poorer...
Til Death Do Us Part

There are times when everyone, even a devout atheist, finds their way to a church; weddings, baptisms and funerals come to mind. Wars, natural disasters, personal tragedies equally fit the bill.

People intuitively sense that some things defy human explanation: the miracle of life, the encounter of love, a lifelong commitment; likewise, the frailty of the human condition, the truth of human weakness, the enduring persistence of human cruelty.

Good or bad, certain experiences supersede our ability to control our circumstances and we long for the reassurance that comes from knowing there is a greater force in charge.

In our Catholic tradition, such moments are often marked by a sacrament, a real and transformative encounter with the living Lord who continues to minister to us today through His body here on earth, the Church.

These church celebrations, however, need not be one-time events. I know many families who mark their children's baptismal day with all the pomp and confectionary excess of a birthday.

Some couples do the same for their wedding anniversary.

Every year my wife pulls out our wedding program--complete with our personalized vows--for our annual renewal of our commitment to one another. We light the unity candle, hold hands and say the words we spoke on that very first day of our vowed life together.

The parish of *Corpus Christi* in Mobile took this idea to another level. They invited all of their parish couples celebrating anniversaries of 5, 10, 15 years etc. to participate in a public renewal and blessing of their marriages.

Of the nearly 50 couples who participated at the Saturday vigil Mass, many were recognizing 50 years or more of marital fidelity.

One inspiring pair boasted 66 years together. The husband lovingly retrieved his wife's walker so they could take their place in the sanctuary with the other couples.

Fr. James Zoghby, the pastor of *Corpus Christi*, invited these couples to face each other as he led them in a renewal of their vows. Many of them fought back the tears. I even felt a lump growing in my throat. I longed to share the moment with my wife but she was in the cry room with my 11 month old. The best I could do was look across the church in the hope that we could lock eyes for a moment.

After the vows, Fr. Zoghby, Fr. John Boudreaux and the congregation joined their voices in a series of blessings for the couples. For those in the marital state who more often than not live out their vocation behind closed doors, it was a great affirmation of the Catholic community's public commitment to marriage.

To top off the evening, an invitation was extended to join the celebrating couples for a reception after Mass, complete with wedding cake and champagne.

The couple next to our table, 5 years married with three small boys, stood up to slow dance as the party began to wind down. With their boys racing up and down the hallway with carefree abandon, this husband and wife danced their way back through the years, recapturing the first embraces of their wedding night. Almost contemplative in each other's arms, they were alone in the romance of their ongoing sacrament.

Our churches are full of activities, programs and events. We do so much for so many different populations. What a treat to see the Body of Christ at its best in prayer, song, celebration, through children, the elderly, the single and the married. Together we all joined in a sort of beautiful dance that night, remembering that with the Lord every moment is meant for a lifetime.

Tips for Everyday Faith

During the Mass celebrating anniversaries, a song entitled "Covenant Hymn" by Rory Cooney introduced this verse which I found worthy of meditation for married couples. "And though you should fall, you will find me. When no other friend can you claim. When foes beat you down or betray you and others desert you in shame. When home and dreams aren't enough, and you run away from my love, I'll raise you from where you have fallen. Faithful to you is my name."

Jesus and the Gas Guy

Last Sunday my wife called me upstairs because she smelled gas. With two babies in the house, we weren't taking any chances and called the gas company immediately. Even though it was the Sabbath, their guy arrived at my door in less than an hour. Not exactly the raising of Lazarus, but for anyone who has spent hours waiting for a service call, you know this was no small miracle.

The gas guy was pleasant and efficient. He discovered a tiny leak in our attic heating unit and promptly repaired it. Grateful for my wife's supersonic nose and this man's professional acumen, I still dreaded the response to my next question: "How much is this going to cost me for a Sunday service call?"

"Oh, for a leak that small, no charge," the man responded matter of factly. "With the holidays coming, that is the last thing you need."

As I walked him back to his truck, I said I would pass the good news onto my wife when I picked her up from church. The gas guy casually commented that he recently took a mission trip to Honduras with his church. Curious as to the details, I asked him where he went and what they did? For the next 20 minutes, standing in front of my house, next to his utility truck, I listened to this man's beautiful testimony about God's action in his life. Without any pretension or bible thumping, he simply shared about his fear of flying and his resistance to joining his teenage daughter on this mission trip.

His eyes lit up when he said that one day he heard the Lord speak in his mind "as clear as day" these few simple words: "It isn't the airplane that you are afraid of." Those couple of words, he explained, were like a "thousand in my ears." To him, the Lord was saying that what he really feared was giving up control of his life and trusting in God completely. Of course it was all true and he knew it. He feared flying, he feared dying. He feared not having enough money and so many other things he tried desperately to control in his life.

As he finished his story, he explained that even though he went to church for years and believed in God, he never really had any personal connection with him before. "Now that is all different. I'm trusting him with my life now and it is such a blessing. My daughter and I hope to go back to Honduras again this year."

We shook hands. I thanked him for the gas service and even more so for his inspiring witness to how God became so very real in his life.

Back in my car, I wondered about us Catholics and how we often struggle to tell our personal stories of the Lord. More often than not we espouse the "go in your closet and pray in secret" (Mt 6:6) style of faith, or the famous St. Francis teaching: "Preach the Gospel at all times. Use words, if necessary."

Quite honestly, few Catholics have developed the disposition or the skill to comfortably share our faith like this gas guy did with me. Scripture says to "always be ready to give an explanation to anyone who asks you for a reason for your hope." (1 Peter 3:15). But we don't like to sound preachy. Besides, most of us believe that in our tradition, the priests and the sisters are the ones tasked to do this type of evangelization.

Is that right though? Are our priests and sisters the only people expected to share the joy that comes from knowing the love of Christ personally? I find that hard to believe. Priests and nuns are not in all the places we are. It wasn't Father or Sister that I called to come fix my gas leak. Yet, it was this simple working man who shared Jesus with me more deeply last Sunday morning than I experience most Sundays with people at Mass.

This call to become witnesses and evangelists cannot remain the sole property of our evangelical, Pentecostal friends. We, as Catholics, are invited out of our closets to sing the praises of God wherever we are, both in our actions but equally with our words when God opens the door.

I'm sure the gas repair man did not arrive at my home expecting to talk about Jesus. Rather, he was willing to tell his story when God nudged his heart and gave him the opportunity. It was a gift for both of us that morning, a gift I pray all of us continue to give to others whenever we can.

http://1bread.catholic.org

This website offers information about how to share your Catholic faith including an Evangelization Kit that you can order.

Games of Faith

A few months ago, we baptized our third child, Joshua Raphael. Since my family lives all over the country, we decided to combine the baptism with our annual family reunion.

All told there are ten grandchildren in my family ranging from 17-years old to our newborn. I didn't realize how much of an impact the baptism had on the little ones until a few days later when I noticed them playing a new game in the pool.

The game consisted of filling up buckets of pool water and dumping them on the younger cousins, ages 2-5. My first reaction to the sight of the nearly drowned toddlers was to yank all the kids out of the pool. But, in a moment of grace, I decided to ask my daughter what was going on before I blew my stack.

"We are playing the baptism game, Daddy," Clare exclaimed as the other kids jostled each other to be next in line, impatiently waiting their turn to be plunged into the pretend waters of salvation.

For the rest of the week, the baptism game ruled the pool. The children simply couldn't get enough of that feeling of nearly drowning in the cleansing waters only to emerge, gasping for air, feeling born again. Their bursting smiles and sparkling eyes told me they got it: baptism meant new life.

Even my younger sister's boys who are not baptized and who have not been brought up in the Catholic faith, lobbied to be baptized over and over again. "I want to be baptized," they yelled. If only they grasped the depth of what they were saying.

I watched poolside from the lawn chair and prayed that one day they would speak those words again in the sanctuary. "What do you ask from the church?" the priest or bishop will inquire. "Baptism," they will respond. From the seeds planted when they were 3 and 4 years old, playing in a pool with their cousins, they will respond: "I want to be baptized."

How we share faith with one another does not always take the form of a witness talk or a bible study. In fact, most of the time, faith is picked up by osmosis, seeping through our exterior only to find a natural home inside our souls where God already lives.

The often quoted aphorism still applies: faith is not taught so much as it is caught.

This past Easter we went to the Easter Vigil mass at St. Dominic church. With two children under 4-years old and a very pregnant wife, it did not seem like a wise decision. I had visions of my exhausted munchkins screaming in the pews and my crying wife begging to be taken home.

But I pressed onward because I had heard that the Easter Vigil at St. Dominic's employed the best of our Catholic rituals, symbols, music and traditions. I hoped that even though the mass would be two hours long, that all the action—the fire, the incense, the full immersion baptisms—would hold my children's interest. And I brought along a few granola bars for my gestating wife in case she had a hunger meltdown.

To say that the children hung on would be an understatement. They could not have been more enthralled if they were on the 50 yard line of the Super Bowl. They loved the powerful symbols of darkness and light. They followed the stories of God's saving history with great interest, especially since the music ministry created animal sounds during the Genesis creation account. We even moved them right up against the baptism font for the hypnotizing site of grown adults being drenched with buckets of water in a big pool inside of a church.

I believe that our liturgy affects us on a subconscious level so that over time we develop a Catholic imagination that sees God all around us. We come to encounter God in water, fire, bread, wine, birth, death, suffering and sacrifice. All the world and all of life become charged with the glory of God. Ritual and liturgy invite us to become a sacramental people, a community that meets God in the stuff of everyday reality.

This mixing of the divine and the human became so clear to me when on Easter Monday I discovered my 2-year old son standing naked in the living room. He was swinging a plastic rope attached to a pair of toy binoculars over his older sister; back and forth, back and forth.

"Toby, what are you doing?" I asked with a sense of impending doom. No doubt he would soon clock her in the head and the mayhem of the day would commence.

"I'm blessing her, Daddy," he nonchalantly explained, never missing a beat in his swinging action. "Just like the priest and the smoke at mass, Daddy." I nearly wept; the incense game.

Life is full of moments of faith and we never know when God is reaching us and those around us. Our Catholic tradition is rich and we have much to share with those in our lives, children and adults, practicing or not.

Tales from the Crypt

I spent one Easter in a cemetery. No, I wasn't exactly visiting the graves of my blood relatives. Nor was I trying to get a part in an episode of CSI. I was at Mass—the Easter Vigil to be exact.

Out in the far right corner of the Archdiocese of Mobile, Alabama is a town called Holy Trinity. There, a little Catholic community founded by the Trinitarian order has a parish church. The Trinitarians also have three cemeteries on their grounds—one for the sisters, one for the priests and brothers, and the one for the public. On Holy Saturday night, I found myself, along with 40 parishioners, there in the public cemetery, standing somewhere between the living and the dead. I'd like to tell you about some of the people buried there as well as how we celebrated the resurrection of Jesus in their midst on that night.

Here lies Leon Domingo—a 23 year old African American from Jersey City, a former soldier. He rests here after being falsely accused of raping and murdering a white girl in 1957. He was executed, just like Jesus, and he chose to use some of his final breaths to forgive his accusers, just like Jesus. His last words as he was strapped to the electric chair were: 'I forgive all of you here who convicted me to death even though I am innocent.' Then they killed him."

Easter Vigil Mass begins with the lighting of the new fire and the words: "...on this most holy night, when our Lord Jesus Christ passed from death to life...(we) come together in vigil and prayer. This is the Passover of the Lord."

Leon Domingo, pray for us.

The priest blesses the Easter candle and reminds us

that the light of Christ dispels the darkness of our hearts and minds. I like the way John puts it in his gospel: "The light came into the darkness and the darkness could not overcome it." (John 1:5)

Here lies Kim Williams —a 22 year old Korean woman who married a US military man. For this, her family disowned her. She moved with her husband to the US in 1976 where he promptly left her for another woman. In grief, she walked the streets of Holy Trinity until one day she stepped in front of a logging truck. No one claimed her body."

Those of us at the Vigil processed up to the Easter candle to receive the light of Christ. The priest then instructed us to ignite the tea light candles on top of each headstone, welcoming into the light of Christ all those among us, even the dead. We read the names, the dates, lit the tea lights and prayed with and for our friends.

Kim Williams, pray for us.

I have never been to Mass in a cemetery. Weird....mystical......powerful. Here it is, the night that Jesus passed from death to life and we were right there with everyone, on both sides of the great divide. The only light we had was Christ. What else could I say but "thanks be to God."

As we processed towards the church through the fields, candles in hand, I felt the presence of the ancient Church. Torches in hand, they too walked and worshiped among their dead, there in the catacombs. Martyrs for the faith—witnesses to the light on the other side.

Inside the church, we stayed among the cloud of witnesses (Hebrews 12:1), remembering in the readings their days on earth with God. Then we asked for prayers, in the litany of the saints, from others who knew the Lord. The crowd of the dead just grew and grew as Mass went on.

How they must have all cheered for the young man who was baptized in the church that night. He was the newest one to join the family, to die in the waters of baptism and be raised to new life, to receive the light of Christ from the Easter candle.

Here lies Kenneth Bearden—a homeless man. He was taken in by a Hispanic family of recent immigrants. They loved him and he loved them. Six months ago, two men, Kenneth and another, were out together. A shot from a gun pierced the night. Maybe it was an accident. No one knows.

Several people that night at Mass received their First Holy Communion. They shared in the body of Christ, the living body that we are, and drank the blood of Christ from the cup that makes us one.

Kenneth Bearden, pray for us.

I started this reflection saying that I wasn't visiting the cemetery on Easter to pay my respects to blood relatives. Now that I think about it, I was wrong. The same blood runs through us all. That blood soaked the cross. That blood forgives our guilt. That blood makes us family. That blood brings us home. *Leon, Kim and Kenneth,* Christ is risen indeed. Thanks be to God. Alleluia!

Postscript

A Korean woman who read this chapter in the Archdiocesan newspaper where it was first published found the family of the Kim Williams in Korea and told them what happened to their daughter. Until then, they never knew what had become of her.

One of Many Choices

The other day I found myself on a street in Mobile, Alabama. The thought crossed my mind: "I could be in any town or any city anywhere in the U.S. and the scene would be relatively unchanged."

The requisite Starbucks welcomed me at the entrance to the avenue followed by a Burger King. A few office buildings dotted the landscape mixed in with a shopping option or two. Finally I noticed the Chuck E. Cheese indoor playground for small children. On this day, Chuck appeared to be the most popular establishment on the block, beating out Starbucks by a mouse's tail.

So many choices, diversions and options in just this one little area.

There was one more option on this street that I haven't mentioned. One more choice someone could consider here in Anytown, U.S.A. You might not even notice it amidst all the options lining this street. Many, perhaps, blindly drive right by it after getting a latte at *Starbucks* or a chicken sandwich at Burger King. This business, just like so many other chain stores and restaurants, is available across our great nation and fits quite neatly into our culture of options, choices and recreational possibilities.

Don't be confused though. Death happens behind this establishment's doors. Not the kind of inevitable bodily death that comes from too many burgers or the spiritual death that comes from too much shopping. This kind of death can only be described as murder.

There, I stood in front of a Planned Parenthood clinic and watched young women and young couples pull into the parking lot with plans to kill their pre-born baby.

Planned Parenthood is the largest abortion provider

in the country. Literally, millions upon millions of lives have been destroyed behind those doors. They don't advertise their product that way as if they were McDonalds with a Golden Arches sign that reads "millions and million served". Imagine a scarlet *PP* with the words "millions and millions killed" below it. Maybe a sign like that would clear up the common misperception that Planned Parenthood is a place where women can go for help.

Certainly, I'm not suggesting that people choose an abortion like they choose a cheeseburger. By all accounts, for most it is an agonizing decision made by people who don't know what else to do. They believe it is their only realistic choice.

The people who were on the sidewalk that morning with me were hoping to provide at least one more option to those couples that day: choose life. With literature in hand and training that disposed us to compassion instead of judgment, we hoped to advocate for both the pre-born baby and the uninformed or desperate parents. Perhaps, if they knew they had a few more choices, they might make a different decision.

One related choice became clear that day, a choice that pertains to both you and me. Those of us who believe abortion should be illegal are asked to provide more than a principled pro-life position. We need to choose a lifestyle of commensurate heroism. In other words, when we say "choose life", we have to back that statement up with action.

Many people who consider abortion a tragic but necessary evil often punctuate their argument by saying, "what are you willing to do to help the woman and the baby if she doesn't have an abortion? Are you going to take the baby?"

Although this argument is unfair, what it does point to is the need for a commitment to a lifestyle of commensurate heroism. In other words, if we ask a woman to make the heroic choice, are we willing to match her courage and sacrifice? Can we offer her commensurate (or comparable) heroism?

Any time in history that lives have been saved, someone provided commensurate heroism. Millions were killed in the Holocaust but some were saved. Or think about when Herod launched his bloody campaign to kill the infant Jesus. His soldiers slaughtered countless innocent babies but we know at least one child survived. How many people must have risked their lives and security by helping Mary and Joseph flee to Egypt? How many lied to Herod's soldiers when asked about the young couple and the newborn baby? They could've been killed. And what about the people who took them in when they arrived, found Joseph work, and helped Mary set up house for her newborn? So many, many people must have gone to great lengths to choose life for that baby boy. I wonder if any of them even knew that Jesus was the Messiah. Maybe they did it for other families and scripture only records that Joseph and Mary escaped. These people, these regular citizens of Bethlehem, they showed extraordinary heroism for the cause of life. Are we not called to do the same?

Maybe we are not in a crisis pregnancy situation, but many people are. Statistics show that 1 in every 8 women in the U.S. has had an abortion. By those numbers, we all know someone who has been, is or will be in this situation. What can we do to help? How can we become the type of people to whom they would turn in this moment of uncertainty and fear?

What about the many people we know, meet or hear about who could use a little help? Do we choose to go out of our way for them? Every sacrificial, noble or virtuous choice builds a culture of life and a community that provides for those in need. Sometimes this means a monetary donation. Or perhaps we can give our time. Maybe we need to get more involved in how our tax money is spent so that our communal funds are used to help, and not hurt, people. The choices are endless.

For myself, too often I get distracted from the things that truly deserve my time and money these days. Starbucks, Burger King, Chuck E. Cheese, work, my favorite shows on TV, the football game. Too many choices, too many diversions. I hope I make the right decisions more often than not. I know I need to do something even if I can't do everything. Standing on that sidewalk, I realized that lives are literally at stake.

www.youtube.com

Type in "99 Balloons Baby" and watch this video with many examples of ordinary people doing their part to affirm the value of human life.

A Catholic Altar Call

Have you ever been flipping channels and stopped to watch an Evangelical revival service on TV? Those people look jazzed. Dancing, singing their hearts out, laughing as they listen to an entertaining preacher, those congregations certainly seem happy to be there.

In many of these services, the preacher inevitably invites people to accept Jesus as their personal Lord and Savior and come to the front as a sign of their decision for Christ. I'm seen it so many times, I am tempted to call it a ritual or even a "liturgy." I know Evangelicals don't do liturgy but it has that predictable rhythm to it.

The whole structure is very different from our Catholic liturgy. In fact, it seems kind of foreign. But I have to make a confession: I often wondered what it would be like to get up and walk to the front. Would I have the courage to stand up? Would I feel the stares of everyone around me? Or would I be so swept up in the moment, so overwhelmed by the sense of Christ's presence that I wouldn't care. "Jesus, you are my personal Lord and Savior," would fill my mind and soul. I could imagine it, but would I do it?

I once went to a Billy Graham Crusade in Madison Square Garden. The music played, the people sang, Billy preached and then... he gave the altar call. Hundreds and then thousands of people came forward. I was amazed. I also never left my seat. The Catholic in me fished through my pockets for my rosary and with my head down, my body still fixed to my chair, I prayed in my heart. To my mind, unless they were giving out ashes, a throat blessing or Holy Communion, I wasn't going anywhere near the front of that stadium/church.

I attended a young adult conference once for work.

The Conference offered all the elements that typically appeal to Catholic college students: clear, straight forward teaching of the faith; young presenters who could articulate why they do more than occasionally attend Mass; lively music; talks on relationships; strong Catholic symbols and opportunities for prayer, Mass and the Sacrament of Reconciliation.

What I didn't expect was a "Catholic Altar Call." On Friday night, after an hour of beautiful singing and prayer, the leader invited those who wanted to "take the next step in their relationship with the Lord" to come forward to the front.

Come to the front? I didn't know what to do.

Here I was, immersed in my Catholic world, with a statue of Mary to my left and a huge crucifix in front of me. We had spent the day hearing talks that quoted the catechism and the pope, referred to the saints and the sacraments. But now, in my comfortable Catholic world, I was being invited to come forward in a new way. No communion line to join, no rituals to fall back on. Simply come forward if I wanted to go deeper with Christ. What was I to do?

I quickly downloaded my internal Google search to find a precedent for this "Catholic altar call"? At once, the image of Jesus telling Peter to come out on the water flashed into my mind. Wasn't Jesus inviting Peter to take that next step in his relationship with the Lord? To go deeper? Then I thought of the many times Jesus said to various people: "get up," "see," "walk," "believe," "eat my body, drink my blood." Was this any different? Was this invitation to do the unscripted, the unexpected, the uncontrollable really outside of our tradition? Didn't I publicly profess my faith every week at Mass in the creed and in my procession up the aisle to receive Jesus—body and blood, soul and divinity—as my Lord and Savior. Yes, yes!!! Amen!! I knew I had to go.

Up to the front, down on my knees, Lord fill my

heart, yes Lord I believe. On my right cried a young woman in a way that reminded me of the woman who washed Jesus' feet with her hair. All around me I sensed a deep communion with the young adults in the room as well as with the great cloud of witnesses who had answered the call before me. I never realized our Church was so evangelical.

I admit I feel closer to our Protestant brothers and sisters now. I can't wait until someone asks me "if I am saved?"

No Plan B

My wife said to me today: "I'm sorry I disappoint you." I was horrified and saddened by her statement. All I wanted to do was hug that crazy idea out of her head. Instead, I insisted that she didn't disappoint me in any way and nothing could be further from the truth. What had I said that she would even think such a thing?

After I left for work, I thought about her words. Of course there are times in our marriage that we have disagreed or acted unloving towards one another. That is normal and to be expected when two adults with different personalities and from different families live for years together in such tight quarters. But we try to not let our hard feelings simmer too long. Usually, following a little sit down conversation where we air our grievances, we exchange apologies, ask for each other's forgiveness and acknowledge our human weakness before God.

The truth is that we are both sinners who are prone toward selfishness. We regularly blow it. But that doesn't mean I am disappointed in her. Mostly, I just am grateful that the Lord loves us despite our deficiencies, that there is grace in the sacrament of matrimony and that my wife made a vow to put up with me. Realistically, marriage is impossible. Add to that the task of rearing children and you could rightly describe the normal family situation as "disappointing" on multiple levels. For every good thing I do at home, I can name at least three occasions when I knowingly or unknowingly chose to take the easy way out. And that is just me.

Case in point: our infant still isn't close to sleeping through the night. When he wakes up at 3:00, 3:30, 4:00 and 4:45 in the morning, I try to lie perfectly still and pretend I am in deep REM sleep. I'm convinced my wife is doing the same thing. Sometimes I could swear she has stopped breathing. Now that is commitment!

Inevitably, our baby's shrieks are impossible to ignore and Rachel nudges me as if to say, "can't you hear him?" I am loathed to get up because I am lazy and selfish. I want her to get up. In fact, I wouldn't protest if she always got up. Not exactly heroic, I know, but it is the truth. And I'm the head of the household, the spiritual leader, the guy with a theology degree and the one who works for the church full time. What is my excuse for such self-centeredness? The bottom line is that we need to maintain realistic expectations of each other and ourselves, practicing mercy, patience and long suffering when necessary.

I look at it this way. Christ came to earth and set things in motion for the Kingdom of God to overtake the world, restoring the original vision of God as seen in the Garden of Eden.

But then the Lord left and put us in charge. Not exactly the brightest move if you work on a Fortune 500 success model. Sure there have been some triumphs throughout the years—a few saints every generation, Catholic hospitals, Catholic schools, our care for the poor around the world, some great art and literature—but are we really that much better than they were in the times of Jesus? Are Catholic people living in such a way that we are clearly identifiable as followers of the teaching and example of Jesus our Lord?

When I seriously assess the state of the world today, it makes me wonder if God is disappointed in us. Have we failed in the charge He has left us? Is He formulating another plan? Or is God a God of mercy, patience and long suffering? Is God rooting for us to succeed but supportive of us when we fail?

The evidence of the bible suggests that God is more than aware of our shortcomings and chooses to entrust us with the great mission of the gospel anyway. With realistic expectations, the Lord is kind and merciful, slow to anger and rich in mercy. With loving kindness, Christ knows we are like sheep without a shepherd and His sacred heart bleeds and breaks for us.

Are we a disappointment to God? Not by God's standards. We may not be perfect or even close to successful in living the exemplary life, but love covers a multitude of sins. That is why marriage is a gift. That is why children are a blessing. That is why God's kingdom will come and God's will *will* be done, through us and with us.

There is no plan B. We are it because we are God's beloved. He has made us a little less than angels, created with the outrageous capacity to act and love like Him, even if it only happens every once in a while. Will we always succeed? Absolutely not. Is God disappointed? Only that we don't believe that He loves us more than any sin we could ever commit.

Lord, release us from the need to perform for your approval. Free us to simply accept your acceptance of us, as we are and not as we should be. You will get us to where we need to be. This we know, because you are in it with us for the long haul. You took a vow in that manger long ago that you'll be right beside us no matter what, till death do us part and even beyond.

Meeting the Pope
Diary Entries of a World Youth Day Pilgrim

"Welcome to World Youth Day." Those were my words to the group of Alabama pilgrims who were gathered around me at the end of our first night of World Youth Day.

We had been in Australia for a week already, serving the local church in Tasmania. But now we had finally arrived in Sydney, joining 500,000 pilgrims from around the world.

I must admit, after weeks of hyping *WYD* to this group, I was a little worried that they might be disappointed, that the event might not live up to their expectations.

At the end of the first night though, looking at their glowing faces, I knew I had nothing to fear.

The night began with us snaking our way through the crowds until we were about 20 rows from the central altar stage area. The energy all around us made the Super Bowl seem like a funeral.

Following a rousing chorus of the *WYD* theme song (*Receive the Power*) and an official welcome by the Prime Minister of Australia, we settled in for the Opening Mass with the Cardinal Archbishop of Sydney. The Mass included Aboriginal dancers, extra verses of every song and an inaccessible communion line. We needed to jump the barricades to receive. That unique Eucharistic experience was quickly dubbed "Jumping for Jesus."

After the two-hour liturgy, we settled in for a picnic dinner with hundreds of thousands of other pilgrims and began the process of meeting the youth of the world.

Excited dinner chatter ensued: "Where are you from? *Tonga.* "Where is that? *Near Tahiti in the Polynesian archipelago.* "Cool. Want to trade hats?"

Stomachs full with Australian lamb stew, the youth spontaneously created the world's biggest street dance party. The scene looked like a staged Budweiser commercial or a scripted *MTV* youth festival, only there was nothing fake or artificial about this celebration. No products to sell, no image to create, simply music, youth and the intoxicating joy of the Spirit of God.

One adult commented: "When do young people get together to have this much fun? Amazing and not one drop of alcohol or any trouble whatsoever. There are police everywhere with nothing to do. This is so beautiful. I wish everyone could see this."

Following a spectacular fireworks display, I rallied the group before heading back to our sleeping quarters. Their faces sweaty, their eyes filled with a light that only comes from God, I knew we had arrived. *"Welcome to World Youth Day."*

I remember my first *WYD*. Not unlike this year, the press predicted small turnouts. Reporters asked why American young people would want to go to such an event; too far, too expensive, irrelevant to irreligious youth and too big an inconvenience for busy teens and young adults. Surprise, surprise. Over 1 million people showed up to pray with Pope John Paul II at the final Mass.

A revolution in the American Catholic church had begun. Those young people, like me, never knew we were part of something that big, that extraordinary, with leadership that inspiring.

There, out in the middle of an empty field, we were given our marching orders. "The Church is counting on you to change the world for Christ," the Pope told us and we believed him. "The Pope needs you." That was all we needed to hear. At last, someone in authority who took us seriously and gave us something worthy of our energy and idealism. Bringing the world to Christ was a task worthy of our best efforts and the best years of our lives.

During the past 15 years, whenever I meet a young priest, a thriving group of youthful sisters, a lay minister whose eyes are ablaze with the love of God, our conversation always includes these familiar phrases: "You were there too....Do you remember when he said....Wasn't the Lord so present there....It was like being in heaven."

Something supernatural happens when the Vicar of Christ gathers the church like that. And when he calls the young people together, the fiery presence of God's Spirit pours out into the streets.

Some memories from my WYD experiences stand out in my mind.

In Toronto, the pilgrims took over the public transportation system. Still, even though a million exuberant strangers might seem intimidating or annoying to the normal commuters, by the week's end, even the hardened businessmen who hid behind the *Wall Street Journal* joined in the cheers and songs. They couldn't resist the spirit of love coming from this international family of God.

In Denver, the garbage men were interviewed after they cleaned up the massive amounts of trash left in the field after the final Papal mass. "Bet you are glad those kids are gone?" prodded the reporter. Their response: "We would do this extra work every day for the rest of our lives if those kids would come back and stay here." Even knee deep in garbage, those men knew they had been given a taste of heaven.

On the bus back to the gym where we slept, the bus driver, a retired cop who was helping the city transport the pilgrims, asked if he could say something to the group. He said: "When I wasn't with your group, I shuttled the cardinals and bishops to their hotel. Over the past year, we have had bloody gang wars in our city and I told the cardinals not to go out the side door because that was gang territory. Yesterday, as I loaded the last of the old guys, I noticed a tiny Asian bishop coming out the side. I could see a group of gang members walking towards him. The cop in me went into high gear and I ran out into the street even though I didn't have my gun. I figured he'd be lucky if they just stole his gold cross and didn't kill him. When I got around the corner, I couldn't believe my eyes. Those punks were on their knees and that little Chinese guy was blessing them. I don't know who you people are. Hell, I don't even go to church. But if you can do that to our city in just one week, you must be doing something right."

Right now, I am sitting in an open parking lot the size of three football stadiums. The praise music is pumping. The Jumbotron is projecting young Catholic singers and dancers from all over the world, providing inspiration and entertainment for the crowds. We are all waiting for the arrival of Pope Benedict XVI.

Right in front of me is a circle of Africans, Asians, Australians, Aborigines, Americans, Canadians, Samoans, Tahitians and Europeans. They are united by their Catholic faith and right now they are kicking a soccer ball between them.

The crowds...oh, the crowds...it is so hard to capture the scene. In every direction, my eyes reach the horizon before I see the end of the gathered Body of Christ. Mostly the people are teenagers or young adults. But there are a fair number of adult chaperones and thousands of religious sisters, brothers and priests.

Sorry. The Pope just pulled up. I need to go. More from World Youth Day next time.

Secular to Sacred
The Journey of World Youth Day

Perhaps it is simply a matter of practicality, an unavoidable accommodation made to absorb the enormous surge of people. After all, there are simply no churches big enough to house half a million people, not even St. Peter's Basilica in Rome.

I suppose a city has to use whatever is available. In Sydney for World Youth Day, the choices included most of the downtown area, the buses, the subways, the Olympic complex, the famous Sydney Opera House, the major city parks, the Sydney bay, the waterways, the convention center, an abandoned shipping port and their horse racecourse. All of these venues metamorphosed from commercial and recreational centers to temples of the sacred, houses for the holy.

Take, for example, the convention center, no doubt the home of many business conferences, professional symposia and twice baked potato banquet meals. But for *WYD*, the major halls were converted into centers for confession and Eucharistic Adoration. From 8 a.m. until 10 p.m., thousands of young people spent countless hours before the Blessed Sacrament in silent adoration, interceding for the world and seeking God's direction in their lives. Confessions were heard around the clock both here and in every corner of the city. Priests who might hear one confession on a typical Saturday afternoon at their local parish were barraged by pilgrims ready to bear their souls and receive God's mercy.

The little used port area named Barangaroo was the site of the Opening Mass with Cardinal Pell of Sydney, the *WYD* opening concert as well as the welcome for Pope Benedict XVI. This makeshift outdoor stadium was designed to house 200,000 pilgrims. At various times, the *Barangaroo* blacktop felt the knees of the praying masses, the stomping feet of the dancing concert goers and the outstretched toes of throngs pressing to snap a picture of the Holy Father as he cruised by in his Popemobile.

A Saturday night prayer vigil and the final Sunday Mass with the Pope were held at the Randwick horse racetrack. I imagined how many times the Lord's name was taken in vain at this place as a horse failed to meet expectations. And now here we were, insisting that this center of gambling and diversion belonged to God as well.

Even those locals who tried to avoid the holy madness of *WYD* might have looked out of their office windows during Friday's three hour Stations of the Cross to see Christ walking through their city streets on his way to Calvary.

The Lord and the Church were simply everywhere you turned.

One local newspaper headline read: "How Will Australia's Most Secular City React to *WYD*?" From my vantage point, it seemed clear. The secular was swept up in the sacred.

Or maybe I should say, the glory of God, which is always and everywhere present, was made obvious for all of us to see.

The theme of *WYD* was taken from Acts 1:8. "You shall be clothed with power from on high when the Holy Spirit comes to you and you shall be my witnesses to the ends of the earth."

Our group of pilgrims certainly felt as if we had traveled to the ends of the earth to partake in *WYD*. Now we need to accept the challenge to be his witnesses back home. The US could use an infusion of the sacred into our secular society too. We need to recognize the glory of God in our streets, our schools, our businesses and our abandoned places.

Stepping onto the final plane on the last leg of the long journey home, a woman in first class recognized my *WYD* hat and greeted me by saying: "Welcome pilgrim." Even in my exhaustion, my heart skipped a beat. I knew the Lord was reminding me that the pilgrimage was just beginning and now it was time to be His witnesses on the other side of the earth.

The Priorities of God

During Sunday mass last weekend, the priest preached a completely inappropriate homily. At least that is what my brother-in-law, Joe, thought. His groans and twisted facial expressions betrayed the volcano bubbling within him. If we were not at church with all our children, he might have walked out.

The topic of this outrageous homily? "Just as Jesus sends the Holy Spirit as our *advocate*, so too we must *advocate* for the priorities of God in the world." Pure heresy of the highest degree.

To be fair, Joe was not reacting to the theological premise of the priest's message, one we could ignore once we left the church as an irrelevant pious preaching. "Yes, yes, we should do the will of God, blah, blah, blah." Rather, it was the example used by the priest that elicited Joe's ire.

Father spoke of a conference he attended on global warming. His point being that from a spiritual point of view, we have to adopt and *advocate* for a way of living in the world that shares the resources of God's creation fairly. More efficient technologies are nice, he suggested, but in the end we Americans will have to change our overindulgent ways and start making sacrifices if others are going to have their fair share.

To illustrate his point, he cited the following data: Americans make up less than 5% of the world's population but consume 25- 30% of the world's resources.

Joe didn't hear a word he said. He was too busy mumbling under his breath about how this priest needs to be censured for preaching politics.

Joe's misunderstanding about the church's role in

the world is not uncommon. We have grown accustomed to the church speaking publicly in defense of the unborn and many Catholics, my brother-in-law included, would welcome a monthly homily denouncing the evils of all things pro-choice. That message matches their political persuasion.

But others cringe at the church's engagement in the public debate over pro-life issues. I still remember a counterprotester's sign I read at one pro-life march that stated: "Don't impose your religion on my body!"

Their misunderstanding is the same as Joe's. It goes something like this: the Catholic Church's teaching, if it supports my personal opinion, is prophetic and a moral voice championing the will of God. If the church's teaching speaks out against my position, then the church is violating the separation of church and state and is becoming too political.

I remember a parishioner who verbally assaulted me on the stairs of the church because I hung up the statement by Pope John Paul II against the war in Iraq. He said I shouldn't be displaying my political propaganda. I inferred that he disagreed with the Pope. You can imagine how difficult it is for our priests to preach what the church teaches when people react like this.

The beauty of being Catholic is that our church's teaching is not beholden to national agendas, political preferences or cultural biases. Catholicism is based on the teachings of Christ, the truths of scripture, the inspiration of the Holy Spirit, natural law and the theological inheritance of a 5000 year relationship with our Father, Yahweh God.

The church is international, intercultural and interdisciplinary. It is as if the church offers a bird's eye view to us normal people who so often are blinded by the biases of our time and place in history.

To truly listen to the fullness of what the church is

teaching on all the hot button issues will and should challenge us all, regardless of our preferred politics. We need the church to help us form our consciences so that we can vote and engage in the tough issues of our day.

It is up to you, me, Joe and all our Catholics to *advocate* for the priorities of God in the world. But we first have to move beyond our tendency to tune out our church leaders because they challenge our politics.

Jesus said "the truth will set you free" but an insightful believer later added "but first it will make you flinch."

The World Is Dripping

I'm sitting on a porch right now with our sleeping newborn in my lap. We are listening to an impressive thunderstorm. My 2-year old son just walked over to announce: "Daddy, the world is dripping." He turns and bounces back inside.

People have commented a lot lately about our third child. "You're not planning to have anymore, are you?" "This will be your last, right?"

Unless you live on Mars, you know that big families are "out" in American culture. Small, manageable, affordable families are in. Big families are simply impossible to deal with these days. Minivans only seat seven. Who can afford to educate all those kids, let alone clothe, feed and accessorize them with all the accoutrements necessary for modern family life? Consider the cost of ipods and laptops alone.

Modern life simply works better with a nuclear family of four: father, mother, son and daughter. Maybe a dog if you can find a good kennel.

The rain is coming down in torrents now, too much for the gutters to flush away. The streets have turned into little rivers. So much precious water simply falling out of the sky. No charge.

My friend told me that family life changes when you go from two children to three. "We used to play man to man," he explained. "Now we play strictly zone."

So far, that image aptly describes our new existence. As soon as the baby stops crying, I discover my son is throwing a ball against the mirror in the bathroom. I ask him "why are you doing that?" He replies, "I dunno." I relieve him of the ball. The requisite tantrum ensues. I punt, turn him over to my wife and walk into the kitchen to pay some bills.

The house is quiet for a nano-second before my hysterical 5-year old daughter comes running into my arms. Evidently, my son dealt with the loss of his ball by biting her.

Zone defense means crisis management. My parenting style has evolved into that carnival game called "Whack-a-mole," only I don't get the stress release of actually clubbing anything with a mallet.

The rain drenches the ground, soothing my mind. My sleeping newborn seems to appreciate the pitter patter of the raindrops hopping on and off the leaves as much as I do. He just smiled. Nature has a way of whispering right past our ears and into our souls.

The idea of a third child concerned me at first. I adore my first two and I wondered if I could love another with the same intensity. Would there be room in my heart (or in our car) for one more? Now that he is here, amazingly, there is not just room to spare but a deep gratitude for the gift of this child.

We hear at Mass and in the Book of Genesis that we are made in the image and likeness of God. Perhaps my baby and this rain are speaking to me of those words. God gives and gives and gives, generous to a fault, lavish in His generosity. The rain comes and comes, drenching, soaking, nourishing, washing, offering relief to a steaming, sweltering world. Then, just as it slows and I presume the vaults of heaven are exhausted, out pours another deluge, deeper and more profound than the first. Is there no end to the abundance of God?

Our spirit, so much like God's, stands capable of supernatural generosity, this pouring out. Life, if we allow it to, invites God-like self emptying. Jesus says the rich reservoirs of our souls are hardwired for heroic self giving, like the genetic code in a grain of wheat. (John 12:24)

Children are one way this unique capacity is unleashed. Crisis, suffering, poverty and self denial can also uncork this divine generosity from deep within our character. These stressors uncover truths about our inner nature such as: We are capable of greatness. Despite evidence to the contrary, there is always room for more. There is more love than we dare to imagine, compassion for the mighty and the fallen alike, and forgiveness for the unforgivable.

On some level, we require blessed chaos in our lives to make room for the holy interference of God.

My world is dripping right now, soaked in the graciousness of God. Disguised as piles of toys, dirty diapers, loads of laundry and unpaid bills, grace pours down upon me, drenching, soaking, nourishing and washing me. My gutters are overflowing. I cannot soak it all in. Such a gift and all for free.

Tips for Everyday Faith

Inconvenience, difficulty and suffering can result in bitterness and discontent. They also can be a doorway to spiritual growth if we seek God in these moments. When you hear those voices in your head telling you how oppressed you are and how unfair your life is, change the channel. Instead, ask God to unleash the power of the cross in your life. Use these trials, these little deaths, to bring out the unfathomable power to love which is already within your soul, compliments of God's Spirit given to us in baptism.

www.vatican.va

In 1994, Pope John Paul II wrote a "Letter to Families" (*Gratissimam Sane*) which lays out the challenges and blessings of family life. His words give encouragement and theological grounding to the everyday tasks of marriage and raising children. My favorite section is entitled: "Love is Demanding."

Let's Sell This Sucker

Barbara Stanton is married 41 years, the mother of two, a grandmother, a resident of Mobile, an award winning realtor, a Roman Catholic, a retired catechist from Corpus Christi parish, a graduate of the Toolen Institute for Parish Services, and a missionary in her everyday life.

The mission field: Roberts Brothers real estate agency and the streets of Mobile. "It can be easy for any realtor to think 'Let's sell this sucker' when you get a small house," admits Stanton. "Or 'this person isn't ready to buy a house right now so I can't waste my time on them.' But I honestly try to treat everyone with dignity and respect no matter what the house size, the price range or the status of the person. Those things don't matter."

What does matter to Stanton is that she takes seriously her role as a realtor. "I do feel a sense of mission in this job," explains Stanton. "I know these people are customers but I think: 'This person has been put into my life and I am going to give them my best. Even if they cannot buy a house right now, I want to teach them how to buy one when they are able."

That type of commitment might seem like good business sense, but the motivation for Stanton goes deeper. "I used to volunteer a lot," recalls Stanton. "I spent years as a catechist and volunteering for many church and community groups. Now I don't do that as much. Still, I bring that experience to my work as a realtor. This is where I make a difference now."

Stanton sometimes struggles when old acquaintances from her volunteer days challenge her about her career. "Most people who know me well, know that money wise, I could stay home and still do volunteer work," offers Stanton. "Some say: 'Oh she just wants to make all this money'. But I believe this is important work and I am still helping, just in a different way."

Other factors weighed into her decision to leave a life of volunteerism and church ministry years ago and enter the workforce. "I wanted to prove that I could do this," she says. "Even though I usually can't talk about my work as my mission, I know this is how I live out my faith."

Her clients attest to Stanton's sense of purpose and the extraordinary effort she makes on their behalf. "Barbara went out of her way for us when we were house hunting," describes Rachel Sodusta. "She became more than a realtor to me and my husband. It was like we had a friend who was an expert in real estate. Even now, we feel comfortable calling her with questions about our new home."

Relationship building, selflessness and personal attention are earmarks of Stanton's work. "I just think about the clients sitting at home waiting, wondering and worrying," describes Stanton. "I know I am tired and I want to go home, but if I make just a phone call or two, I can give those people peace of mind. That is worth a little extra on my part."

Stanton brings this selfless style into her position as a top realtor at Roberts Brothers. "I teach a class for new realtors many of whom enter the job thinking this is just a business," illustrates Stanton. "I try to show them what it can be. I want them to remember that the elderly widow who is selling her house—that is the last house she will ever own. That's hard." "Or the excitement of a young pregnant couple," she continues. "This will be their first home, the place where their babies are born, the place that affects so much of their lives. Who will their children play with? Who will be their neighbors be? What memories of Christmas, birthdays and First Holy Communion parties will they make here? A house holds a lot."

This sensitivity and wisdom comes out of her own journey with life, loss, God and homes. "I remember when my mother died," she reminisces with sadness. "It was more gut wrenching for us to sell that house than to say goodbye to Mom. We knew her death was coming and had time to prepare. But to leave that house where we all grew up, it meant we would never go back again. We stayed up until 2 a.m. that last night."

Recently a family of immigrants from Afghanistan became Stanton's clients. Because of her reputation for offering compassionate and quality service, Stanton often receives referrals for clients with special circumstances. This family was one of those cases. The mother, a widow with four children, could not speak any English. Stanton admits it was difficult.

"They wanted this house that had a pool," she recounts. "I tried to talk them out of it because they didn't know how to care for a pool, but they bought it anyway. So I took them to a friend who owned a local pool shop. I knew he would not take advantage of them and sell them useless chemicals."

These may be little things, she knows, but they matter to her clients. "My job is not to perform miracles everyday but I do feel called to do this work as a follower of Christ," she states. "That means that whenever I can, I do the right thing and take care of the people."

And the kingdom of God, which is like a tiny mustard seed, takes root at Roberts Brothers because of missionaries like Barbara Stanton.

A Broken Marriage

The teachings of the Catholic Church on children and contraception are clear according to the Catechism:

"Fecundity is a gift...for conjugal love naturally tends to be fruitful. (2366) Called to give life, spouses share in the creative power and fatherhood of God. Married couples should regard it as their proper mission to transmit human life and to educate their children; they should realize that they are thereby cooperating with the love of God the Creator and are, in a certain sense, its interpreters. (2367)

For just reasons, spouses may wish to space the births of their children. (2368) ...methods of birth regulation based on self-observation and the use of infertile periods, is in conformity with the objective criteria of morality. In contrast, every action which...proposes, whether as an end or as a means, to render procreation impossible is intrinsically evil: Thus the innate language that expresses the total reciprocal self-giving of husband and wife is overlaid, through contraception, by an objectively contradictory language, namely, that of not giving oneself totally to the other." (2370)

In this context, I listened to a friend, Agnes, recount her ongoing struggles in her marriage to Jake. Since marrying Jake less than five years ago, Agnes has conceived and delivered four children.

"After the fourth baby," Agnes explained, "Jake announced that we needed to change our family planning. He wanted to be a good father and husband, and he couldn't see how that could happen if we continued to have more children. In short, he was getting a vasectomy."

Both Agnes and Jake are committed, practicing Catholics who orientate their lives around God and the Church. Agnes has even worked in various Church ministries since before their marriage.

Clear about the church's teaching and the sinfulness of something as drastic as birth control through surgery, Agnes dug her heels in.

How could she be an authentic witness to the gospel, "if within my marriage, I was no longer open to life? How could I minister to other women and encourage them to be bold in their faith if I wasn't living it myself? And what do I teach my children about marriage and sex when their father and I weren't aligned?"

She admitted: "At first, I cried. Then I yelled. Then I argued, calmly and intelligently. Then I cried some more. I shared with my husband excerpts from Kippley's *Sex and the Marriage Covenant* and the encyclical, *Humanae Vitae*. We listened to Christopher West and Scott Hahn in the car. I reached out to every resource I had, but my husband was unchanging."

After fighting a quiet battle over this for a year, she explained, "we were exhausted. One night, I cried through the night. At 5:00 a.m. there was a sudden and unexpected thunderstorm. In my mind, the raindrops were God's tears and I sensed the Lord was with me. Then I heard in my ears -- as if God had a human voice – the words, 'I am in a broken marriage too.'"

From that moment on, Agnes told me, her attitude changed. "I thought about how much we--the Church, the bride of Christ--hurt our Lord. How we ignore Him, dishonor Him and behave in ways that do so much damage. And yet, He never holds back. He comes to us, over and over again, giving us his body without bitterness or manipulation. His love remains faithful and unchanging."

Agnes resolved after that to try to be more like Christ in her marriage.

"I can't change my husband and in many ways, I don't want to. He's an honest, strong, loving man and father. I would never choose another. All I can do is keep my vows to love and honor him all the days of my life; to give myself to him and lovingly receive him, just as Christ does with His beloved, the Church."

She concluded: "To destroy our marriage would have meant killing the life we have been given. So instead, I offer it up. I lift up our marriage, our intimacy, and our continued conversion to God who knows our hearts and our failings, and who loves us with a perfect love."

Tips for Everyday Faith

If you are facing problems in your marriage, seek the wisdom and counsel of God by prayerfully studying scripture and Church teaching. Also, consult your pastor, a spiritual director or a Catholic counselor. For more help, check out Retrouvaille ministry at http://retrouvaille.org.

A Plea for Peace

For over one hundred years Catholic Social Teaching (CST) has embraced and proclaimed the inaugural words of Jesus: The spirit of the Lord has anointed me (us) to bring glad tidings to the poor, the blind, the captives and the oppressed (Luke 4:18). Only recently, though, has the Catholic community begun to recognize the central place of peacemaking in this mission.

This call to peacemaking can be seen from that very first Easter. On the night of the first day of the new Eden, the risen Christ appeared to the disciples, stood in their midst and spoke the words of resurrection fulfillment: "Peace be with you, my peace I give you." (John 20:19; 14:27). "...(Jesus) showed them his hands and side...and said to them again, 'Peace be with you. As the Father has sent me, so I send you.'" (John 20:20-21).

From this seminal moment, Christ's mission of peace was transferred to us: establish the Kingdom of God and proclaim the good news of God by the promotion of peace. Peacemaking is at the heart of the task for which we are sent to all the nations. It is that into which we baptize people—the very peace of Christ.

CST draws from a rich tradition of responding to social injustice in each generation. Catholic social thought, beginning with Pope Leo XIII's *Rerum Novarum* in 1891, took concrete shape as a set of seven principles gleaned from encyclicals and other episcopal statements. These principles proclaim the vision of the Kingdom of God in the face of the complex social problems. Abortion, human trafficking, globalization, environmental degradation, child labor, health care, faithful and active citizenship, and fair trade are a few current issues that are fundamentally challenged by the vision of CST. How we as North Americans live in the global community comes under harsh scrutiny when measured by these principles.

But it seems that the trajectory of CST has not yet reached its logical conclusion, the conclusion of the Risen Christ that first Easter day, the conclusion of "Peace." Is there a principle in CST that does not depend on peace and at the same time promote that same peace? When the dignity of the unborn, the aged and the infirm in our midst is disrespected, is it possible to see the humanity of the Iraqi people underneath our 25,000 megaton bombs? When human labor is a commodity exploited for a $1 savings at Walmart, are we likely to embrace sweatshop workers in China as our brothers and sisters in Christ? Or are they simply tools that support our affluence, to be demonized and killed when they seek justice for their labor? Will terrorism ever cease when entire communities, ravaged by war and its effects, live in squalor and desperation? Will the goods of creation ever be justly distributed when billions are spent annually on the weapons of war?

CST begs for an eighth principle: Peacemaking. Historically, the Catholic Church departed from its gospel stance of nonviolence with the legitimization of Christianity by the Roman Empire of Constantine. Augustine of Hippo, in his attempt to challenge unethical and unregulated war-mongering, unwittingly entrenched the Church's acceptance of violent statecraft with his theory for a just war. Sixteen centuries later, hundreds of wars fought, millions killed directly and indirectly, the Church has yet to break ties with the myth of redemptive violence. Not one war fought has been "just" according to the Just War criteria *(jus ad bellum* and *jus in bello)* and yet the followers of the nonviolent Christ continue to kill and be killed on the front lines, with the dutiful Church liturgically petitioning for their safety.

Politicians co-opt the language of a "Just War"

because the Church lacks a clear statement against all war to eliminate divergent interpretations of what makes a war "just." Consider the *War in Iraq*—a "just cause" according to President Bush. This conflict publicly pitted prominent Catholic theologians and commentators against the Vatican's principled condemnation of preemptive war. For many involved in these debates, it was a matter of perspective, left to the vagaries of personal and political interpretation. The language of "Just War" lent itself to easy manipulation without a serious commitment to the principle of peacemaking. Does not the Spirit that anoints us cry out for a stance on peacemaking that provides the prophetic clarity the world needs?

In 1983 the US Bishops' *The Challenge of Peace* began the process of challenging the militarism of the world. That document, giving little attention to peacemaking, critiqued the arms race and nuclear war through the lens of the Just War Theory. Twenty years later, the US bishops, following the lead of Pope John Paul II, proclaimed that war is never the solution and that we must plot a path to peace. However, despite this positive movement, the Church still lacks a clearly articulated principle committing itself to peacemaking and nonviolence.

For many, a hard stance on peacemaking makes the Church irrelevant in conversations about international politics, easily brushed aside like the Quakers or the Mennonites. But to assume that our place in the US and the world can be so easily ignored contradicts the fact that Catholicism has a voice because of our presence everywhere. We are too numerous to be ignored and we are no longer a disempowered, immigrant Church. We are politicians and lawyers, teachers and social workers, parents and priests. We are in every country and in every sphere of society. We are even 375,000 strong in the US military. What we lack is a clear statement upon which to galvanize our people power.

Without a principle on peacemaking, all of CST limps. Without a commitment to peacemaking, children will continue to learn war as our society and Church offer no other relevant career paths for those who wish to solve international unrest. Without a call to heroic sacrifice for peace, our heroes will die on the battlefield, guns in their hands. The time is right to invest our vast Catholic human, institutional and financial resources towards the cause of peacemaking. No excuses, no exceptions and no apologies. The nonviolent revolutions over the past century in India, Eastern Europe, the Philippines and South Africa confirm the power of nonviolent resistance.

This stance for peacemaking will not come without a cost. On that first Easter evening, Christ's words were "Peace be with you" but he was quick to show his disciples the scars that peacemaking brings. Nonviolent resistance requires tremendous courage and an unwavering belief in the rightness and effectiveness of nonviolence. People will die and tremendous sacrifices will be required. But don't people die now in our wars and are there not tremendous costs being paid by the all parties involved? Moreover, to actively engage in peacemaking will bring the wrath and violent opposition of the war industry and those who believe that violence and superior weaponry will save us. We must challenge the false gods of war and align ourselves with the nonviolent Jesus we worship on the cross.

CST provides a spinal column for Catholics and "people of good will" to confront the heavy load of so many imbedded systems of sin. The burden is weighty and unmanageable apart from the yoke of Christ. But we believe that the Spirit of the Lord anoints our unwilling flesh and opens unforeseen vistas of international solidarity, reconciliation and cooperation. As Pope John XXIII wrote in *Pacem in Terris,* "Peace on earth, the profound aspiration of men and women of all times, can be firmly established and sustained only if the order established by God is firmly respected." And what is God's established order if not for us to live in peace with one another.

It is time to believe the words and witness of the Prince of Peace. It is time to act with the conviction of the apostles and the early Christians who laid down their lives rather than cooperate with the violent machinery of the Roman Empire. To do so is to accept our commission from Christ and be sent to profoundly and prophetically promote peace, standing in vulnerability and solidarity with those most in harm's way.

A Modest Proposal for Parish Life

In a good number of churches around the country, parish life is characterized by activity. Open up a large parish's bulletin and you'll often see groups that gather for every age and interest. In many ways, this is a positive development.

Yet, for all this activity, Mass attendance continues to decrease, many feel disconnected from the Church and even some who do attend Sunday liturgy find the experience to be cold and somewhat void of personal interaction.

Is the answer more programs, services and activities? "No," according to Brother Bob Moriarity, S.M., a leading voice for the renewal of parish life through NAPRC, the National Alliance for Parish Restructuring into Communities.

"For priests, staffs, lay ministers and key volunteers, parish life over the past 50 years has become a recipe for burnout," states Brother Bob.

He continues: "Parishes can become seduced by needs, find the itch and scratch it. The vital parish of the new millennium will be enamored not just be fulfilling needs but by relationships, with God and with one another.

But to get to relationships, we need to slow down, connect with one another, sift and sort through the things that count, to be present to how God is acting in our lives," he suggests.

Since parishes, in general, are not set up to allow people to hear each other and connect faith to life, the question is: how to do this?

After traveling around the U.S. and the world, researching the practices of the best Catholic communities, Brother Bob makes this recommendation to help regular people connect God to their ordinary life:

Every time people gather for any reason outside of liturgy, take a few moments-start with 5 to 7 minutes-and pose of question for consideration. Allow for a minute or two of silent reflection and then invite people to exchange their thoughts with the person next to them.

For example, at a Confirmation parent's meeting, ask "what did you have to go through to get here tonight?" Allow for silent reflection, then conversation. Finally, gather everyone's reflections and offer them to the Lord in an opening prayer experience.

"This is not heavy, touchy feely, bare your soul, when were you most naked before God, stuff," Brother Bob explains. "You simply honor people's lives and bring them to the Lord. It is out of their lives, after all, that they come to the church. It is out of their lives that they will minister."

This kind of basic silence, connection, conversation and prayer establishes a grammar in faith sharing. In time, when people become comfortable with this practice, the Sunday gospels can be used as the focus for reflection. But even with the gospels, the questions must still connect to everyday life.

Imagine all the situations this practice can be used in parish life, this basic grammar of connecting life to faith.

For the ministry group that is struggling: "Name one time when this ministry has been life giving for you."

For the parish staff: "What excites you about your work right now?"

For catechists and teachers preparing their children for Christmas break: "Besides the gifts, what do you want for you and your family this Christmas?"

For a group of senior women in the parish: "Think of a child in your family that you are concerned about right now. What is your prayer for them?" Silence, then share.

For the music group: using the words of a new song,

pose a question, allow for silence, conversation in pairs, and then prayer.

One pastor dared to try this at the annual CYO sports awards dinner where he was asked to say grace before the meal. He stood up in front and asked: "Besides winning or losing, what has it meant to you to be a part of this team together?" He gave them a minute of silence and then invited them to turn to the person next to them and discuss. Some of the über jock Dads couldn't handle it so they stood up and started filling water glasses throughout the banquet hall. But everyone else joined in. After a few moments, the pastor re-gathered everyone and suggested that they take all their thoughts and bring them into the grace they were about to say together. Later, after dinner, when the coaches took the podium to present the awards, several mentioned what they thought of before grace.

What would be the cumulative impact of this approach if it were employed over time in the life of a parish every time people gathered?

Brother Bob says, "Imagine if people said: this is not what we do when we gather, this is who we are. We are silent, we reflect, we connect with one another about what's going on, and we honor the presence of God in our everyday lives. Then we bring it to the Lord in prayer."

No new programs, tasks, services, responsibilities, or ministries. Simply 5-7 minutes every time people come together; time for silence, connection and prayer. Is that so radical?

Is This What
We're Supposed to be Doing?

Ok, so I go to work, come home, go to work, come home. Drive the kids to practice for the Christmas play. Kiss my wife as she rushes out to the next thing. Catch her words as she flies down the driveway. Evidently, there is a list for me on the kitchen counter.

The dishes are still in the sink from this morning. Before we know it, the time has come to pick up the kids. A late dinner, a little homework, carry the baby while my wife punches out a priority email and then we are into the bedtime routine.

Even after the kids are down, three hours of work lie before us. We hope to be in bed by midnight.

The thing that bothers me is that I know it all starts again tomorrow. In fact, the weeks, months and years are blurring together these days, obscured by the onslaught of daily tasks that never get conquered but instead seem to breed somewhere in the back room of our house.

Wasn't it just yesterday that we were on our honeymoon, the world lie before us and we were dreaming about all the great things we could accomplish together? Now, married with four children, a mortgage, leaky faucets, a house begging for a paint job, stacks of administrative work piled up on my desk, I wonder: "Is this what we're supposed to be doing with our lives?"

Already, we see the window closing as we reach our forties. Where did our youth go? The years are flying by so fast. Did we miss something along the way?

My sisters are farther down the road than us. They have children in high school and college. When we talk, they are asking the same questions. We commiserate in our shared search for answers and meaning in the midst of the daily doings of family life.

This morning I awoke at 3:00 a.m. My daughter's baptism is scheduled for 10:30 a.m. The list of to-do's is racing through my mind, disturbing my sleep. I try to calm my thoughts, breathing deeply, fixing my focus on the Lord, offering my little girl into His loving arms. I feel the tightness in my hands recede and I slide into a half conscious state, somewhere between distraction, peaceful slumber and meditation.

My mind recounts the story my wife told me earlier in the week. She is holding our baby girl who is playing Jesus in a live Nativity scene in front of our church. A man approaches my wife. Not a parishioner, he appears shy, awkwardly slow and a little bit off. She is cautious at first but notices the innocence in his eyes. He asks her in all sincerity: "Can I see the baby Jesus?" She watches in awe as his face beams with profound joy, staring at the holy child, our daughter.

At the baptism, I look around at the room full of friends, parents, grandparents, godparents, children, children, children and a baby dressed in a white gown. The dress is made of fabric given to us by a women we know who lives on a garbage dump outside of Mexico City. She presented us with the material as a gift for sponsoring her daughter, who died of multiple sclerosis. Somehow, I imagine her questions about the meaning of life are different than mine. For her, all of life is a gift and she is grateful, even on a garbage dump, even though her daughter died. I pray that her spirit characterizes our family in the years ahead.

On the baptismal font sits the bowl that carried the Eucharistic bread at our wedding. A friend made it for us as a wedding gift. It has been the basin for the baptisms of each of our children.

The priest prays over us that we would be good parents to our daughter and help her know the Lord's love for her. Surrounded by God's grace, we feel more like lottery winners at that moment than the overwrought couple we thought we were a week ago.

At the little reception in the parish hall, my wife's mother and brother sing "O Holy Night" followed by a trio of spiritual songs performed by my older kids, songs they learned at all those play rehearsals I drove them to night after night. They sit on a table and belt out in full voice: "I'd rather have Jesus than silver and gold." My sisters wipe the tears from their eyes and smile at me.

I'm not sure what I thought we were supposed to be doing with our lives but when I pay attention to what we are doing, I'm tempted to say these ordinary, mundane, every day, monotonous demanding elements of family life might just be holy.

I doubt the history books and the *New York Times* will seek to immortalize 99.9% of our lives. But God is paying attention and I'm starting to think God is doing something extraordinary, even if we are too distracted, busy and preoccupied to notice most of the time.

Football, Catholics and Mass

Football is big in Alabama. REAL BIG. The Auburn Tigers, "Roll Tide", the Iron Bowl, even the high school games are events across the state. I cannot say I completely understand the phenomenon, being weaned on pro sports in the North. But I appreciate the devotion.

My only point of reference comes from my years at Notre Dame. Because of the Fighting Irish football team, South Bend – a little town in Indiana where corn and cows outnumber people – becomes the center of the universe for a half dozen Saturdays a year.

Nearly 90,000 people descend on this tiny village and engage in what can only be called a "liturgy". Like our Catholic Mass, the entire experience is a scripted ceremony of public celebration. A few examples will serve to elaborate.

On home football Saturdays, the drum corps from the pep band leads an opening procession called "Step Off" an hour before the game. Starting from the stairs of the Golden Dome Main Building (with the signature statue of the Blessed Mother on top), the drummers lead thousands of fans through the campus to the stadium. A regular repertoire of songs, chants and cheers are intoned while the procession passes the sacred football art on campus: "Touchdown Jesus" and "First Down Moses."

Once at the stadium, all "Domers" (Notre Dame students and alumni) know their role in the communal experience. They know when to sing, sit or stand and what to say in response to the leaders (of cheer). They say: "We Are" and 90,000 strong scream in unison "N.D.". It is wonderfully similar to what happens at Mass when the priest says "The Lord be with you" and we all respond "and with your spirit."

There are even announcements at the end of the game. I suppose the collection happens beforehand at the ticket counter.

The sense of belonging and community is palpable, even for visitors. The "liturgy" at Notre Dame lets you know that you are part of something bigger than yourself, part of a tradition that includes parents and grandparents, legends and heroes, triumph, tragedy and championship. Every week the Notre Dame community regathers to share the experiences of the week, pour out its hopes and fears, and finally dream of a promised land. Nothing changes from year to year, and you can always return because you are part of the family.

It may seem trivial because it is only football, but for "Domers" it is a deep expression of who we are. "We Are N.D." And this is what we do.

Of course ritual and tradition are not the sole property of Notre Dame or Catholics. At Auburn, they have the Tiger Walk, rolling Toomer's Corner and the flight of the eagle before home games.

In Tuscaloosa, there is the Walk of Champions, the Rammer Jammer Cheer and a requisite visit to the "shrine" of the patron saint of Alabama football, the Bear Bryant Museum.

And for all sports fans, there is the joy and fellowship of sharing a greasy meal and a cup of spirits in the parking lot before and sometimes after the game.

Rituals, especially in a community, have great power to provide identity and belonging. Catholics have known this for centuries and we cherish our traditions for this reason.

To be Catholic is to understand that we come together to worship at the table. We collect our sacred art, sing our common songs and lean on our ancient traditions. We are saints and heroes, sinners and screw ups. We share life and death, defeat and victory, devastation and sublime ecstasy. And in the end, there is always next week to regather and reaffirm our belief in the promised land. We may not get there today but together we know where we are headed.

Christian Tree Huggers

Doesn't sound like words that belong together or fit the same people, but you might be surprised. Christian environmentalism is on the rise.

It wasn't long ago when environmentalism was considered a dirty word among conservative Christians and even in some Catholic circles. Visions of paganism, hippies and anti-free market protests leapt to mind. Political caricatures of environmental activists painted a picture of rogue secularists who sat on the fringe of the economy, the American capitalistic culture and even the church.

That caricature is hard to maintain though when Catholic bishops, recent popes including Paul VI and John Paul II, and 86 leading evangelical ministers including Rick Warren (author of *The Purpose Driven Life*) come out with public statements calling for intentional environmental activism by Christians. Even Pat Robertson recently said that people are heating the planet and something needed to be done. The current Holy Father, Benedict XVI, is so vocal about the environment, he has been labeled the 'Green Pope' by the international press.

Listen to this from the U.S. Bishops in 2001: *"At its core, global climate change is not about economic theory or political platforms, nor about partisan advantage or interest group pressures. It is about the future of God's creation and the one human family. It is about protecting both "the human environment" and the natural environment.[1] It is about our human stewardship of God's creation and our responsibility to those who come after us."* Global Climate Change, #6

Or from the world's bishops at the Second Vatican

Council: *"God destined the earth and all it contains for all people and nations so that all created things would be shared fairly by all humankind under the guidance of justice tempered by charity."* The Church in the Modern World #69

Or Pope John Paul II: *"The dominion granted to man by the Creator is not an absolute power, nor can one speak of a freedom to "use and misuse," or to dispose of things as one pleases. The limitation imposed from the beginning by the Creator himself ... shows clearly enough that, when it comes to the natural world, we are subject not only to biological laws but also to moral ones, which cannot be violated with impunity."* On Social Concern, #39

Gone are the days of relegating the topic of creation to the first two chapters of Genesis or to St. Francis and his bird bath. The Catholic world is waking up to what the Church officially calls "Stewardship of God's Creation." (See www.osjsm.org/cst for the major themes of Catholic Social Teaching.)

Of course this makes some people nervous. It brings Catholics into the public arena on a subject that many would like to divorce from people of faith. Catholics, when informed, profoundly influence the public debates in this country. Look at the effect the concerted efforts of pro-lifers have had on America's attitude toward abortion over the past 33 years. Imagine the powerful voice Catholic and Protestants could have for the environment. United in a biblical vision of God's created order, we just might stump the pollsters and their narrow definitions of what Christians ought to care about.

Christians around the world are waking up. Perhaps economist Fr. William Ryan is right: "We are discovering today that our growth-based economy is already hitting against external limits such as clean water, fresh air and nonrenewable resources, leaving most economists and many scientists in a state of denial."

But like our battle for the lives of the unborn, this battle will be arduous and filled with conflicting politicized voices. Public confusion could make inaction easier than listening to the clear voices of our Catholic pastors and shepherds. Just think about how often we don't even recycle out of laziness or that "story" we once heard about how "they just throw it all into the regular garbage anyway".

Perhaps we need to hear the challenge from those people who seemed like such radicals just a few years ago. Calvin DeWitt, a Christian environmental activist since the 1970's, forced me to rethink my comfortable opinions when he said:

"We've spiritualized the devil. But when Exxon is funding think tanks to basically confuse the lessons we're getting from this great book of creation, that's devilish work. We find ourselves praying to God to protect us from the wiles of the devil, but we can't see him when he's staring us in the face."

A Saint. Who, Me?

Someone said to me once: "The only point of this life on earth is to become a saint." Sounds good, doesn't it? I was inspired and I liked the idea of saddling up next to St. Francis, St. Teresa of Avila and a few of the other heavy hitters.

But then I looked at their lives and what they did in light of how things were turning out for me. I wasn't a priest or a brother. I was a college educated professional employee who worked in an office. I wasn't single or celibate. Rather, I had a wife and small babies for whom I needed to provide. I didn't live in a religious community with a vow of poverty. I lived in a house, with a mortgage and a never ending list of things that needed attention. Sainthood according to many traditional categories seemed less attainable than ever.

I want to dedicate my life to prayer and to the poor, becoming a champion of justice for all the downtrodden. But honestly I often don't even feel comfortable rolling down my window when someone with a sign is begging off the side of the road. Sometimes I think I am just supporting their addictions. Sometimes I am just scared.

Sainthood? Well, maybe I could shoot for heaven even if I would probably have to settle for the cheap seats.

Recently a friend of mine pointed out a strange line in the Bible. God says in Genesis 1:26: "Let *us* make man in our image, after our likeness." My friend asked me, "Who is *us*?" When he answered that the *us* in that verse was the Trinity, I felt silly. "I knew that," I told myself.

Oddly though, that line has stuck with me and in an unexpected way, it has reopened the door to sainthood for us mere rank and file believers. How? Here are some thoughts:

God in Godself is a community, a family. And we are created in God's image and likeness, to be in community, to be a family. Therefore, in as much as we isolate ourselves, become self absorbed, preoccupied, individualistic, concerned with our own needs, in as much as we do that, we distort, destroy and deform the image of God which we are made to be. Why? Because God is always about totally giving His love away for free, just as God does in the Trinity—Father to Son, Son to Father, Spirit to Son and Father and so on. And then, Father, Son and Spirit give to us and all of creation.

Conversely, in as much as we live for others, give ourselves away, put others first, deny ourselves so as to have more for others, live simply so that others may simply live, and die to ourselves for the good of those who deserve it and even for those who don't deserve it. In as much as we do that, we are becoming more and more the person God dreamed about when God created you and me; in the image of God.

To be like the Trinitarian God is what we call holiness or sanctity. But this is extremely hard for most of us so God implemented "a get holy whether you want to or not" program called "Family Life." Family life is God's trick to make us holy.

We grow up as kids, totally self centered. Then we become teenagers, young adults and start to think more about others. But of our own volition, very few of us would willingly do what it takes to deny our desires, squash our egos, die to ourselves and become the saints God planned us to be. That's like giving up ice cream for Lent and then moving into the ice cream aisle of the supermarket for the next 40 days. Impossible. Who could survive?

But God is smart, he gives us a desire to mate—to find that special person with whom we will share passion, intimacy, transparency, commitment and a lifetime of unending pleasure.

So we seek this person and find this person and marry this person and much to our shock and horror, we realize that this person is God's way of making us holy. This person will make you a saint because they will teach you to love, compromise, forgive and die to yourself whether you feel like it or not.

They are your personal saintmaker. But don't laugh, you are their saintmaker.

And just when you start to get a handle on how you can control the unwelcome demands of marriage, God introduces part two of the "Get Holy" program: children. First one baby, then maybe two, three or more. And these little bundles of joy, who eventually grow to be teenagers, are specialists in saintmaking. They force you to live for someone other than yourself. All the control you once believed you had is long gone and you learn the saintly art of trusting the Lord completely.

Family life is the crucible through which God molds us into saints. We all have families and we all know how demanding those relationships can be, married or not. It is a genius plan and we can live it without having to join the Franciscans or move to Calcutta.

My wife says that when she is home with the kids she is feeding the hungry and clothing the naked (Mt 25). That's not bad.

The call to sainthood is simply the call to love. Family life helps us get beyond our self imposed limits because, like it or not, these people are our family and we are stuck with them even when we don't feel like being very loving.

God's call to family and community takes on many forms throughout our lives—friends, roommates, extended family, co-workers, parish life, neighbors, the global community. But the bottom line is this: the only point of this life on earth is to become a saint. Saints love like God. Do you know anyone who needs your love?

Tips for Everyday Faith

Look at your spouse or your children while they are sleeping. Bless them and pray over them. Recall those moments of great joy with them and thank God for the gift that they are in your life. Then tell them you love them when they wake up. Follow that up with a short but thoughtful affirmation note stating all the reasons you love and respect them. You'll be surprised what it will do to you and to them.

José Crow Laws

I am a minority, the son of a Hispanic immigrant who left South America and moved to New York City in the 1950's. After marrying my father, my mother's legal status in this country regularized and she became a US citizen.

All this being said, if I were to be pulled over because of a broken tail light on an Alabama highway, I have nothing to fear. I look white.

My wife, however, is often mistaken to be a Mexican even though she is Filipina. Plenty of people test their Spanish on her, assuming she's an immigrant.

When she read about Alabama's new "toughest law on immigration", she responded: "Great, I better not forget my wallet because they can throw me in jail now for not producing proof that I am American."

In response to the law, a group of 2,500 U.S. citizens from churches across Birmingham marched in silent protest carrying candles and ringing bells. The impetus for their public demonstration? They wanted to stand alongside the strangers in our state whom Jesus insists we welcome. (Mt 25:35) By the way, the march was organized by rank and file Catholics, many of whom have never marched for anything in their lives. They had studied the church's teaching through a parish program called JustFaith and the experience compelled them to put their faith into action.

The fact that our national immigration policy is deeply broken is not a matter of debate. It is. The right of a sovereign country to defend and control its borders is also not a contestable point. We all agree on that.

What is at stake these days is whether this country, with Alabama leading the way, will adopt laws that are purely punitive towards a vulnerable population of people. Are these strangers who come from south of the border not our brothers and sisters in the Lord, partakers of the one bread and the one cup which we call Holy Communion? (cf 1 Corinthians 10-12)

Church teaching speaks strongly in support of protecting the rights and dignity of those who migrate seeking a better life for themselves and their families. (www.mdcathcon.org/ immigration)

Pope Benedict XVI states: "All, therefore, belong to one family, migrants and the local populations that welcome them, and all have the same right to enjoy the goods of the earth whose destination is universal, as the social doctrine of the Church teaches. It is here that solidarity and sharing are founded." (World Day of Migrants and Refugees, 2011)

The Supreme Pontiff continues: "It is thanks to (the Eucharist) that the People of God includes "every nation, race, people, and tongue" (Rev 7:9), not with a sort of sacred power but with the superior service of charity. In fact the exercise of charity, especially for the poorest and weakest, is the criterion that proves the authenticity of the Eucharistic celebration" (cf. John Paul II, Apostolic Letter "Mane nobiscum Domine", 28).

Pope John Paul II struck a similar chord saying: "[the universal common good] includes the whole family of peoples, beyond every nationalistic egoism. The Church recognizes this right in every human person, in its dual aspect of the possibility to leave one's country and the possibility to enter another country to look for better conditions of life" (Message for World Day of Migration, 2001)

Archbishop O'Brien from Maryland recently wrote about the racist nature of the current immigration debate and the need for Catholics to challenge ourselves with this question:

Would we happily welcome immigrants to our

country if they were here legally?

I wonder how many of us have formed our opinions on immigration based on politicians or TV and radio personalities rather than the gospels and our own Church's clear teaching. I know I find it hard to hear the voice of the Lord amidst all the noise in our culture.

Still, after so many years of justifying Jim Crow as necessary for the wellbeing of our community, shouldn't we be a little careful that we aren't now supporting José Crow laws?

www.justiceforimmigrants.org

This website is part of the U.S. Bishops work to advocate for a just and humane solution to the issue of immigration in our country. Click the Parish Kit on the right for a great primer on what our church teaches. The sections on "the Economy" and "Myths" are very enlightening.

What Does God Want?

Have you ever asked that question? Maybe you have when faced with a major life choice. For example, should I marry this person? Should I become a priest, brother or sister? Is this the right career move for me and my family? Are we ready for a baby? How do I best care for my declining parents? Is this the right school, major, house, neighborhood, or retirement community? *What does God want me to do?* The question is equally legitimate for less dramatic decisions.

People often fear the implicit "high stakes gamble" of this question. They wonder: What if I misinterpret God's message? What if I do something God doesn't want? Will I be miserable my whole life, doomed by my decision? Is there only one right path? Do I get a chance to start again if I make a mistake? What if I correctly hear God and God asks me to give up something I want? Wouldn't it be better not to ask?

For many, the problem isn't a lack of direction but a lack of trust in God's love for them personally. They doubt that God has their best interests at heart. Without a deep trust in God's loving concern, it is intimidating to ask the question "what does God want?" But with intimate knowledge of God's love, a person is eager to ask this question because he or she knows that what God wants is ultimately what he/she wants—to be happy, fulfilled, loved and at peace.

Matthew Kelly, the Catholic author and speaker, states that this question is THE question of our lives. He claims that seeking what God wants is the only way we can discover the best version of ourselves—the person God dreamed we would be when we were first created.

How, then, do we find out what God wants? In the

Catholic tradition, we call this process "discernment"--the conscious decision to sift through the information to best find where the Spirit of God, the Spirit of truth, is leading.

Spiritual writer Sr. Joyce Rupp describes discernment this way in *The Star in My Heart*: "A movement from the head to the heart, for it is in the heart that wisdoms are born. I can know and experience many things, but they remain only knowledge until I allow them to sink into the depths of my heart, there to toss and to turn, to weep and to wail, to leap and to dance. Sophia (the Spirit of Wisdom) helps me to take facts, data, events, experiences, down into my spiritual womb. There they sit in me, gestate, and are transformed into truths which are eventually brought up into the light of my consciousness."

Here are a three tools for discernment: 1) Pray--through scripture, Eucharist and solitude; 2) Seek counsel--from spiritual directors/companions, wise friends, family, and great spiritual masters; and 3) Have patience—in God's time, God will make all things beautiful.

Finally, a few nuggets of wisdom from those who have gone before us.

1. Befriend failure—we learn more from it than we do from success.
2. Avoidance of pain is the path to stagnation.
3. Choosing includes losing—you always have to give up something.
4. There comes a time for a leap in the dark.
5. Get out of town--travel, get away from where you are comfortable, known and in control.
6. The Lord speaks in the cry of the poor—spend time with the most vulnerable and the least powerful. There you will meet Jesus (Mt 25).
7. Becoming who you are is your true vocation.
8. God speaks in deep desires.

9. Be open to all options—give God a chance to surprise you.
10. There is no such thing as a pure motive—stop waiting for one or you will never move forward.
11. Nothing can separate you from the love of God
12. There is no substitute for experience.

Blessings on your adventure with the Lord.

www.spirithome.com

This basic website includes many nuggets of spiritual truth worthy of our consideration.

Tips for Everyday Faith

Find your passion in life and pursue it. Too often we slip into thinking that life is simply joyless drudgery and sacrifice. Passion, though, is a gift from God meant to lead us to where God wants us to be and where we can best build the Kingdom of God. Face your fear of risking your security. Try something new. Challenge yourself. Pray, discern and step out in faith, trusting that God is with you whether you succeed or fail.

Rachel and the kids out for a hike in the woods.